MINIMALIST MINDSET

Minimalism Habits & Mindsets to Declutter Your Life, Retake Your Personal and Financial Discipline, and Make Your Passions A Priority to Achieve A Better Life!

By
Jenifer Scott

© Copyright 2019 by Jenifer Scott - All rights reserved.

This book is provided with the sole purpose of providing relevant information on a specific topic for which every reasonable effort has been made to ensure that it is both accurate and reasonable. Nevertheless, by purchasing this book you consent to the fact that the author, as well as the publisher, are in no way experts on the topics contained herein, regardless of any claims as such that may be made within. As such, any suggestions or recommendations that are made within are done so purely for entertainment value. It is recommended that you always consult a professional prior to undertaking any of the advice or techniques discussed within.

This is a legally binding declaration that is considered both valid and fair by both the Committee of Publishers Association and the American Bar Association and should be considered as legally binding within the United States.

The reproduction, transmission, and duplication of any of the content found herein, including any specific or extended information will be done as an illegal act regardless of the end form the information ultimately takes. This includes copied versions of the work both physical, digital and audio unless express consent of the Publisher is provided beforehand. Any additional rights reserved.

Furthermore, the information that can be found within the pages described forthwith shall be considered both accurate and truthful when it comes to freely available information and general consent. As such, any use, correct or incorrect, of the provided information will render the Publisher free of responsibility as to the actions taken outside of their direct purview. Regardless, there are zero scenarios where the original author or the Publisher can be deemed liable in any fashion for any damages or hardships that may result from any of the information discussed within.

Finally, any of the content found within is ultimately intended for entertainment purposes and should be thought of and acted on as such. Due to its inherently ephemeral nature nothing discussed within should be taken as an assurance of quality, even when the words and deeds described herein indicated otherwise. Trademarks and copyrights mentioned within are done for informational purposes in line with fair use and should not be seen as an endorsement from the copyright or trademark holder.

TABLE OF CONTENTS

Introduction 1
Chapter 1 *Minimalism And Happiness* 2
Chapter 2 *Living Life By Principles* 10
Chapter 3 *Reality Check* 18
Chapter 4 *Getting Started* 26
Chapter 5 *Financial Freedom Through Minimalism* 34
Chapter 6 *Decluttering The Digital* 42
Chapter 7 *Living With A Non-Minimalist* 50
Chapter 8 *Traveling Light* 58
Conclusion 66
Description 67

INTRODUCTION

Congratulations on purchasing this book and thank you for doing so.
There's only one thing that's needed to live a life that is simple, yet perfectly filled with contentment and happiness. Get rid of everything that is unnecessary. It may be the integral step that is needed, but you'd be surprised at just how difficult many people find this step to be.
Sifting through your belongings, deciding what stays and what goes can be a bittersweet experience, maybe even stressful for some. Going through each item that you own and asking yourself the one fundamental question all minimalists do - do I really need this? - Is going to be more time consuming than you anticipated if you don't have a plan, let alone know where to begin.
Before you begin yanking stuff off your shelves and out of your closets, you need to understand what you're getting yourself into by familiarizing yourself with what minimalism is going to entail. Minimalism is about being intentional with what you allow into your life and what you surround yourself with. It is a tool which is about teaching you how to live your life with purpose and intention, focusing on what you value most in your life by removing the material objects which are distracting your focus.
Minimalism is going to free you from the chains of the modern "clutter culture" that we live in by reminding you that true happiness lies not with your belongings, but in the relationships and experiences that you have. It reminds you that happiness isn't waiting for you at the department stores, but at home where your family and your friends are.
For far too long we have subjected ourselves to rushing from one task to another, putting in longer hours at work at the expense of spending time with our loved ones or pursuing our passion, struggling to stay on top of all our bill payments yet somehow falling deeper into a debt cycle we find it hard to get out of. Minimalism is about to change all of that, and the following chapters are going to show you just how to do it.
There are plenty of books on this subject on the market, thanks again for choosing this one! Every effort was made to ensure it is full of as much useful information as possible, please enjoy!

CHAPTER 1
Minimalism And Happiness

Looking around your home, all you see are piles of stuff around you. You find yourself spending far too much time searching for things around your house, even though you were sure you knew right where you left it. Searching among piles your stuff, you occasionally get frustrated because it takes far too long to find what you're looking for. Sometimes during the search, you come across items you don't even remember you had. Does this sound all too familiar?

If you answered yes, then you've got far too much stuff. Having a mess around the home is one thing, but far too much clutter could be drowning you. Every home tends to get messy every now and then, but when you've got clutter, its constant presence could be stressing you out more than you realize.

Why Too Much Clutter Could Be Drowning You

Most people are drowning in their own clutter and they don't even know it, piles of letters, mail, and magazines in one corner. Papers, documents, and stacks of books in another, expired food in the fridge. Closets bursting full of clothes, some of which you may not have worn in over a year or even forgotten about. Old shoes, furniture that needs repairing but you haven't quite had time for, so they are stashed away in the corner of your garage. Souvenirs and mementos you've had since your childhood, gifts you've received over the years but never used.

Chances are that there is at least one area (if not more) around your home that is just piled with far too much stuff. When you look at that pile, you don't even know how the mess accumulated to that extent. Why does it seem so hard to constantly try and stay on top of the material possessions that we own? And yet, we keep buying even more stuff to add to the growing mess. For many, having clutter around the home comes down to the simple process of too much stuff coming in, not enough going out.

There could be several reasons why you're drowning in your own clutter, the first being that you simply don't put things away where they belong. How many times have you walked in through the front door and tossed whatever it was you were holding at the nearest available spot? Did you stop to ask yourself where the item truly belongs? Getting into the habit of haphazardly chucking things in random places around your home and then forgetting about them is how clutter keeps accumulating. We have limited space around our homes, and it can be difficult to place items away when there really is "no proper home" for them to go. Every item around your home should have a designated "home", which can be difficult if all your free space is being taken up by items you don't even need or use anymore.

Cleaning is not exactly an activity to look forward to, and when you procrastinate and keep putting off cleaning the mess around your home, that's how clutter starts to build. The bigger the mess, the longer it is going to take you to clean. A 5-minute cleanup is now going to take 2-3 hours to get done when the mess has grown far too big.

Your home is like a boat on the ocean, and the clutter is the water that keeps filling up that boat until you eventually sink to the bottom under the weight of it all. You are responsible for the clutter that is in your life, especially when you keep buying stuff that you don't necessarily need. Every time that you add even more stuff to your home, you're filling your boat a little more. Not enough clutter going out and far too much clutter coming in will eventually sink you right down to the bottom. You don't want to wait until that point before actively doing something about it.

The problem is that most people don't realize just how negatively impacted they are by the chaos and disorganized mess that is going on in their lives. It's only when you start getting rid of all the unnecessary things that you begin to see and feel what a difference it makes. If you feel that your life is surrounded by far too much clutter, how many of these negative impacts are you already experiencing?

- **You've Lost Your Motivation** - Just thinking about cleaning the mess in your home leaves you feel overwhelmed that you lose your motivation entirely, and that lack of motivation is now starting to affect the other areas of your life.
- **You Find It Hard to Get Anything Done** - Productivity can be low when you're distracted by all the mess that is surrounding you. Not just at home, but at work too. A messy cubicle and work desk can make it hard to get anything done, even more so if you spend far too much time looking for items because you can't find them among the mess.
- **You Feel Lethargic and Tired All the Time** - Being constantly stressed out tends to do that to you. You may think you're not stressed or bothered too much by the piles of clutter you see around you, but subconsciously you are. Some people just look at clutter and automatically feel tired at the very thought of having to work through the mess and clear it up.
- **You Hold Onto the Past** - Holding onto clutter is the same as holding onto the past. You find it hard to let go of some items, even when you know you should, because of the sentimental value and memories which are attached to it. Sometimes you don't even want to get rid of it because it was a gift and you're worried about hurting the other person's feelings. You know you're never going to use it, but you hold onto it anyway. Holding onto items that are no longer of any use to you is only going to keep you from moving forward because you can't look ahead when you're constantly looking back.

- **You've Lost Your Sense of Purpose** - Clutter has a way of affecting you mentally and physically without you even knowing it. Being surrounded by disorganization makes it hard for anyone to concentrate. When it becomes impossible to have clarity in your life, you begin to question and wonder what you're doing with your life.
- **You Procrastinate More Than You Should** - Clutter encourages procrastination. When you're constantly putting off clearing and cleaning up until "tomorrow", that kind of thinking is going to develop into an unhealthy behavior pattern which is going to extend into other areas of your life, and procrastination is never a good habit to have.
- **You seem to Experience More Disharmonies** - Clutter has been known to be the cause of many arguments and squabbles amongst family, friends, roommates, and coworkers. If you are the one who is responsible for the clutter, being nagged or pressured into clearing it up is going to aggravate you and that will spark an argument. If you are the one who is having to live or deal with a messy individual, on the other hand, you will be the one constantly chasing after them to clean up after themselves, which is still going to aggravate you anyway and spark an argument.
- **You Feel Depressed Looking At Your Mess** - When all you see is mess surrounding your life, you can't help but sometimes feel hopeless, wondering how it came to this. These feelings will be amplified over time if nothing is done about the clutter, and as it grows, so too do your feelings of misery and despair.
- **You've Forgotten What's Important in Life** - Clutter and mess are nothing but a distraction, taking your attention away from what you should be focusing on in your life. The time and the hours that you spend cleaning up could be put to better use doing something productive, something that is going to bring you one step closer to your goals. Clutter distracts you from what's important in life, taking up more of your attention and time.

For all of these reasons and more, a change for the better is needed. That change is minimalism.

What Is Minimalism?

It is an approach which is going to help you reclaim your freedom. If you're yearning to be free from the feeling of being overwhelmed all the time, free from the feelings of guilt, stress and worry, free from feeling like you're constantly trapped in a cycle that you can't get out of, minimalism is the tool that is going to open that new pathway towards a better, lighter, freer and happier you.

There is nothing wrong with having material possessions. We all need to have some items to live a comfortable life. It only becomes a problem when we start to attach far too much meaning to our belongings that we forget about the truly important things in our life, the things that money can't buy. The relationships you have with your family and friends, your good health, gratitude for the many blessings that you have, your passion, your goals, and your dreams, the desire to grow and become all that you can be. Those are the things that matter the most, and when we become far too caught up in materialism, these other aspects are often forsaken.

Owning a couple of material possessions that bring you true happiness is perfectly okay. Minimalism is just the tool that is going to help you be more conscious, more deliberate about the things that you do bring into your life. It is about clearing away all the other unnecessary, non-essential items in your life so you can make room and space for the items that bring you true joy. It is about freeing yourself from the burden of being weighed down by the unnecessary mess to make way for a life filled with more meaning and organization. It doesn't just involve clearing the physical clutter, but the emotional and mental clutter too. Minimalism is about clearing away the distractions to focus on what's important.

Your home would look a lot different without all the unused items which are taking up space. Imagine living in an environment that is simple, clean and with lots of free space and surfaces. Imagine opening your closet doors and being greeted with a view that is simple and stress-free, where clothes are not being cramped and squished together and piled haphazardly on shelves. Doesn't that image seem a lot more pleasant? What about a schedule that is less cluttered and filled with only the very important tasks and appointments instead, which leaves you more free time to focus on doing something for yourself? Doesn't that sound a lot better?

Minimalism is a concept which extends to almost every aspect of your life. It's not just limited to cleaning out your home or your work station. Minimalism even extends to relationships, where you only maintain and keep meaningful and important ones. It even extends to your daily schedule, where you focus on doing less and having a schedule that is not as cluttered as it normally would. Doing less, but everything that is on your schedule is going to be something that is both productive and important.

Minimalists live their lives a lot more efficiently simply because they save a lot of time by having less to deal with. Less clutter means less time spent organizing and cleaning up. Fewer possessions mean less time being distracted. A lot of people are hesitant at first to take up this approach because the very thought of having to part with your belongings - sometimes A LOT of belongings - can be terrifying. The idea of living with less is not something a lot of us are accustomed to. What if this lifestyle isn't what you thought it would be? What if you need to get rid of items that you are not using, but love far too much you couldn't bear the thought of giving them away?

It is okay to have those fears. You're about to begin a new lifestyle change, some concerns are bound to happen. The beauty of minimalism which you will come to realize is that there are not fixed rules which determine the way that you live, none at all. There is not one way or one approach that you absolutely must abide by. The way you live your life as a minimalist is going to be entirely up to you and what works best for you. You can be a minimalist and still have an expensive car. You can be a minimalist and still own a Mac, a house and an iPad. If you need all those items to live and survive comfortably, there is absolutely nothing wrong with owning them. You can still have all those things and call yourself a minimalist. Find what works for you.

Minimalism doesn't mean tossing out almost everything that you own before you can call yourself a minimalist. Minimalism simply means living only on the necessities. It means having one car instead of two. If one car is more than enough for you to survive comfortably, it means owning one iPad instead of two if one is all you need. It's about owning 10 items of clothing which you love and use all the time and getting rid of the old, barely used ones that don't even fit you properly anymore. That's minimalism. Downsizing and simplifying instead of overcomplicating and cluttering.

As you prepare to begin, it is important to note one thing. Reducing the material belongings that you have does result in minimalism, but it is not minimalism itself. Donating and getting rid of a lot of things that you don't need any more doesn't automatically make you a minimalist. It is just one aspect of minimalism, not the entire thing. To truly begin embracing this mindset and this approach to life, minimalism calls for reassessing what your priorities are. Your priorities are what are going to help you get rid of the excess and anything else that doesn't bring value into your life, including relationships. Minimalism is about getting in touch with what's important to you so you can invest more time and effort into it for greater happiness. This mindset is meant to show you that physical and material possessions don't bring you nearly as much joy as you thought it did initially.

Minimalism is going to encourage you to take a deep-dive into reassessing what your passions, your dreams, and your goals are. It is going to encourage you to shift your focus and invest your energies into your passion and the things that matter. Getting rid of the material possessions is just one part of the journey, and the more important part of the process is making the transition towards focusing on your priorities and coming to the realization that life could change for the better when you're not focused on the wrong aspects.

The transition to minimalism is going to be a difficult journey for many. We are all attached to at least some of our possessions, and getting rid of them is going to be a hard task. If you find yourself struggling with this part of the process, take some time to process and figure out what items are worth keeping and which are okay letting go of. The amount of possessions you have at the end of your decluttering process is not what matters, as long as the ones which are left behind are enough to let you lead a happy life. Some people are happy owning less than 100 items, while others may need 150 items to keep them happy.

Before you begin to declutter, it is important that you remember not to get rid of stuff simply because you can, or because you're beginning this new process. Going overboard and clearing out everything that you can without stopping to think about whether it is worth getting rid off could lead you to throw out something that you might actually need or love. When you get rid of something and then realize later on that you actually needed it, you're going to have to go out and spend more money buying a replacement. Money - which you could have saved instead because buying a new item was unnecessary if you still had the old one. Decluttering can be a very emotional phase of the journey, and you should take your time working through the process instead of rushing for the sake of getting it over with.

A good approach to begin easing yourself into minimalism is to test the waters first before launching yourself completely into the process. If you cleared out your bookshelf and kept only a few essential books which are needed or make you happy, don't get rid of the cleared books immediately, but rather store them away somewhere for several weeks. If at the end of several weeks you find that you were perfectly happy living without those books, then you know that you can live without them. If you can live without them and still be happy, then it's okay to either donate them or toss them. This way, you give yourself time to adjust and if you find that there's still something in the pile that you cleared away which you need, there's still time to salvage the situation.

One of the most liberating benefits that come with being a minimalist is how these now freed-up resources can be then applied to the other areas of your life. Owning less stuff means saving more money since you're not spending as much, which then leaves you with more money to spend when there is something which you genuinely need. You wouldn't need to scramble to find the resources anymore because you already have them on hand.

Why Become a Minimalist?

Because you don't want to spend the rest of your life being controlled by a life of excess consumerism, clutter, distractions and just far too much going on. Money and belongings will never be able to buy or bring you the kind of lasting happiness that you seek, and if you continue to chase after the wrong things in life, all the good things in life may just pass you by before you have a chance to grab onto it. You could own everything your heart desires and still feel like something is missing, or that life is incomplete.

That feeling is not going to go away, not until you learn how to focus on the meaningful aspects of your life which have nothing to do with how much you own. Minimalism is appealing to you right now for a reason, and that reason is that you seek something more.

In fact, have you ever thought that you might already be a minimalist without even knowing it? You could already be displaying tendencies towards minimalism if you do any of the following:

- You have empty sections or rooms in your home that are clear and unused.
- You don't have a lot of debt because you don't spend more than you make.
- You don't feel the urge to buy something every time you're in a department store.
- You've been spring cleaning, donating and getting rid of items for a while now and you're perfectly comfortable doing it.
- You don't hold onto unnecessary items, even if they were gifts from friends or family.
- You can't stand the sight of clutter because it drives you crazy.
- You are inspired by stories of travelers who can spend months on vacation with nothing more than a backpack.
- You've been curious about the concept of minimalism ever since you heard about it.

The Incredible Benefits Which Minimalism Brings

For almost every action and decision we make, we hope to get some benefit out of it. If you decided you wanted to change the way that you live, you're doing it because you want to reap the benefits that come with this change. That's why they call it a change for the better, and one of the greatest benefits that come with living life as a minimalist is the lasting happiness that this mindset is going to bring. At the end of the day, there is nothing that we want for ourselves more than happiness. All the material possessions in the world are not going to mean much if happiness still seems to elude you.

Minimalists are happy because they base their happiness on the number of things that they own. Their happiness comes not from belongings, but from life itself, and it is entirely up to them to determine what's important and what's going to make them happy. Minimalists have found that this lifestyle has helped them eliminate discontent by focusing on what matters most, reclaim their time and taught them to live in the moment. This approach has helped them pursue their passions and reconnect with their goals in life once again because they're not distracted by buying the latest car or the latest iPhone model which has just been released. They know that those aren't their goals anymore and thus, they are focused on creating a more meaningful life experience instead.

Other benefits that come with being a minimalist include:

- Helping you get out of debt by consuming less and saving more.
- Connecting you with work that you love by focusing on your priorities and keeping materialistic distractions at bay.
- More time for yourself to do something meaningful instead of spending that time cleaning or running from one task to another by focusing on the tasks that matter instead.
- Less mess, less stress.
- Cleaning becomes quicker and easier.
- You can always find what you're looking for around your home.
- Efficiency and productivity levels increase.
- Greater peace of mind when you learn how to focus on what matters most.
- An increase in self-confidence which comes from relying on yourself instead of being reliant on your belongings.
- Less fear of failure when you're not constantly worried about losing your material possessions because you no longer associate happiness with items.

If you know anyone who has embraced minimalism, they will be able to tell that the benefits you stand to gain will go far beyond anything that you could read about or hear about. It is one of those experiences that you need to live to see first-hand what a difference it is going to make.

CHAPTER 2
Living Life By Principles

Minimalism offers a unique perspective for those who follow this approach to living, teaching with a message that a life that is spent pursuing meaningful experience is a life that is far better than one spent chasing material possessions. This is a completely different approach than the one we have become so accustomed to, a life where we have grown up constantly surrounded by advertising messages which remind us we will never be enough without the latest product or gadget.

Buy this watch and you will be happy. Buy this car and all your dreams will come true. You are not complete unless you have this or that. It is never-ending, and the social media society which we are living in today is doing nothing to help the situation. Advertisements like this constantly push perfectionism through possessions, delivering subliminal messages that we need to constantly keep buying, buying and buying in order to fill our lives with happiness. In a world like this, we have completely lost sight of the simpler things in life that bring even more joy than any gadget or car ever could. In a world like this, we need minimalism now more than we ever have before.

Unlike what those advertisements want us to believe, we don't need a lot of things to be happy. True minimalism finds happiness in having less in order to be able to give more. Minimalism is here to remind us that we are good enough just the way that we are, despite what those advertisements say. We are perfectly capable of being happy even without the latest of everything. A life where far too much time is spent checking your notifications, checking your emails, picking out your clothes or spending even more than you should on something you don't need is not a life where you will find the happiness that is going to last a lifetime.

The very word "minimalism" may imply "less", but this approach to living offers you more than you realize. More clothes, more shoes, more watches, more cars, more collectibles aren't going to make you happy. More freedom, more time, more room for what's important, better health, less worry, more time with loved ones, more time spent pursuing your passion. That's where lasting happiness resides.

The Principles of Minimalism

Minimalists don't live their life by a set of rigid rules, but they do have a set of principles which provide them with guidance on how to make the most out of this concept. Among the basic principles which all minimalists abide by are:

- **Omit Needless Items -** This is going to be the primary principle and the constant theme which keeps resurfacing as you make

your way through the rest of this book. Omit needless items, not every item that you own.
- **Identifying Essentials** - Minimalists are clear about which items are essential for them to live a happy and comfortable life. They select their items based on what's important to them, what makes them happy and which of their belongings is going to have the biggest impact on their lives and their careers. If the item serves a purpose and a benefit in your life, then don't get rid of it just yet. Minimize the number of times you check your emails in a day so you have more time for yourself. Arrange fewer meetings and more meaningful quality time with friends and family instead.
- **Everything Counts for Something** - Everything that a minimalist chooses to keep around in their life counts for something. Every item that they choose to maintain is one that is worth holding onto, and you must be clear about what those reasons are.
- **Be Filled with Joy** - As minimalists work hard to declutter their life from the unnecessary, they work just as hard to fill their lives with something which brings them meaning and joy. Spend time with your children, reconnect with old friends, take that vacation you've been wanting to for so many years, take up a new hobby, discover a new interest, anything that puts a smile on your face, fills you with excitement and brings you joy is worth spending a little bit more time on.
- **It's Not the End** - There is no end to minimalism, and when the decluttering process is over, it doesn't mean it's over. Minimalism is an ongoing process, and you're going to constantly be revisiting and observing your life, determining what else can be done to improve.
- **Everyday Is a Mindful Day** - Practicing mindfulness and awareness of their surroundings is how minimalists stay focused and grateful, finding joy in the little things in life. A simple get together with an old friend is something to be grateful for when you are mindful about how happy it makes you feel. Finding some unstructured time for yourself at the end of a busy week is something to feel happy about when you are mindful of how much this is helping you relax and unwind. Decluttering your calendar is something to be grateful for when you are mindful that it is freeing up more time for you to focus on your passions instead. Minimalists find a lot of reasons to be grateful and happy throughout the day, and it begins with practicing mindfulness.

How a Minimalist Approaches Life
There is an old Zen proverb which goes something like this:

"There was a horse galloping down the road, and it seemed like the man on the horse had somewhere important he needed to be. Another man standing alongside the road asked "Where are you going?", to which the man on the horse replied "I don't know. Ask the horse!"

Reflect upon that proverb for a minute. Does it resonate with you on some level? That feeling that life is somehow controlling you, and you have lost control of the direction in which you are headed. You always seem to be in a hurry, rushing from one appointment or task to the next, but you have no real sense of purpose about what you're doing or where you're going. A life where you have lost control is one you cannot find contentment and happiness.

A minimalist approaches with the realization that if we only have so much space to spare, why would we let that limited space be occupied by the things that don't matter? This helps to put a lot of things in perspective, and the secret to how they find happiness in owning so little. Minimalists approach life by reminding themselves:

- **It Doesn't Need to Cost Money to Be Happy** - When you no longer attach meaning to the things that you own, the pursuit of happiness no longer lies with objects which are going to end up costing you money. It doesn't cost anything to spend time with your family. It doesn't cost you anything to spend time laughing and catching up with friends over good food and a few drinks. It doesn't cost you anything to meditate and unwind after a long day. It doesn't cost anything to be surrounded by people that you love and who love you in return. And all of these things will add more value to your life than anything you could ever buy in this lifetime.
- **They Are Not Static, They Are Dynamic** - You grow, you adapt and you change. You don't remain static for the rest of your life, and neither does minimalism. The lifestyle is going to adapt, change and grow right along with you. The way your life looks right now as a minimalist is not going to be exactly the same 10 years later, it is a process that is dynamic and constantly changing, never static.
- **To Pursue, But Don't Forget** - One of the main themes of minimalism is focusing on and pursuing your passion and the things that bring you joy. However, life does go on and there are still things that need to get done daily for survival. Minimalists go about their day like everyone else, waking up each morning, managing their families, heading off to work, coming home and then repeating the process. These other aspects of life need to be pursued for survival, but minimalists don't allow themselves to forget to pursue what matters too.
- **It Is the Intentional Purchases That Matter** - Minimalists know that it is their intentional decisions and choices that matter

at the end of the day. Even with the purchases that you make. It is not about restricting yourself to what you can or cannot buy, but rather making intentional and mindful decisions about why you're making your decisions and how it is benefitting you to do it.
- **It Is About Making Life Simpler, Not Easier -** Don't fall into the trap of thinking minimalism is going to magically take away all of life's troubles and make it easier because it isn't. Minimalism is about living a simpler life, which may make the difficult parts easier to handle. It is about creating simplicity to be able to handle the bigger challenges when you're not distracted by the unnecessary in your life. Minimalists make room in their life by removing the clutter so they can contribute more meaningfully.

What You're Going to Require to Begin Living like a Minimalist

With simplicity being a key theme of minimalism, being content with everything that you already have is a good requirement to start with. You can declutter and strip yourself down to the bare essentials and necessities, but you will never truly be able to rid yourself of the clutter in your life for good if you don't first learn to be content with what you have.

A lack of contentment will lead to the habit of constantly buying more things each time you feel dissatisfied, which is not what minimalism is about. The root cause of your need to purchase is because you are discontent with what you have right now. That's why you found yourself continuously buying things that you don't need, and the more you have, the more you just seemed to want. You constantly want more fun, more excitement, something greater, something better, something cooler. Nothing will ever be enough, and there will always be reasons to remain unhappy if you're not content with what you have, even though it is more than enough to keep you happy.

Which is why the very first requirement of minimalism is contentment, think about what it is that you genuinely need right now. Food, water, a roof over your head, clothes to keep you warm. A family, friends who care about you, a stable job helps pay the bills, a phone that works to keep in contact, a computer that works to help you get your job done. If you've got all that - you already have a lot to be grateful for. The latest gadgets and technology, the most stylish clothes, new pairs of shoes, a fancy car that you can show off, a bigger house that boasts your success, those are not essentials, nor are they necessities. You don't need those to be happy.

To begin living like a minimalist is also going to require that you put a stop to buying anything that is considered a non-necessity. Understandably, this is going to be a challenge if you have never done it before, and a great approach to help you through this process is to create a 30-day list for yourself, and it works wonderfully well at curbing impulsive spending and buying. From this moment on, each time you want to buy something that is considered a non-necessity, put it down on your list. Write down the date next to it so you know how to keep track once those 30-days are up. Keep that item on the list for the next 30-days, and if by the end of that you still have a strong desire for it and you've got the funds to spare, go ahead and make that purchase if it is going to make you happy. This is an effective approach to take because you many times you will find that your urge to purchase dissipates by the time those 30-days are over, which means you never really needed it to be happy anyway.

Minimalists have made it a requirement for themselves to learn how to be happy by doing instead of owning. It is absolutely possible to be happy living with only the necessities once you learn how to be content and realize you already have all that you need. When you focus and turn your attention instead to doing things which you know are going to make you happy instead of buying things which you think are going to make you happy, the need for stuff is going to fade away over time. Once you reach a certain point, there will be nothing left to buy anyway.

Minimalism is going to be a big change in your life, and good change like this isn't going to just happen overnight. You're not going to decide today that you want to embrace minimalism, wake up the next morning and find that everything has fallen perfectly into place. Like all good change, this is going to take time, and the consciousness of it all is the key to making the biggest difference. Being conscious of the needs vs. wants, the more vs. enough is going to be what helps shift your consciousness towards contentedness, which therein lies the foundation of what minimalism is all about. Socrates once said, "the secret to happiness is found not in seeking more, but by developing to enjoy less".

When you put your necessities into perspective, eliminating the non-necessities becomes an easier process. When you start to realize that you don't really need a ton of clothing when you don't wear half of it, it's easier to get rid of it. When you realize that the gadgets you have now are more than enough to get the job done and keep you happy, you don't need to go out and get more. A lot of the things which we think are necessary are not necessities. One of the problems that we are faced with is that we tend to categories our belongings as necessities, and that's because we are so used to having them around that we never thought we could live without them.

Like your car for example. We often see cars as necessities because they make our lives more convenient, but are they really a necessity? Surprisingly, they aren't, especially when there are lots of people out there who are surviving just fine without them. If you live in a location where decent public transport is easily available, that makes surviving without a car much easier. Public transport, not to mention rideshare options are abundantly available in most cities, and if you feel like getting in some exercise, you could always consider riding a bike instead of owning a car.

Something else that we think of as a necessity is having a closet full of garments. But do you need a closet that is bursting to the brim? You don't need to own lots of clothes, and if you are one of those people who only rotates between a few pieces of clothing which you feel most comfortable in, you'll quickly realize how true this is. It is possible to own just half the clothing that you have in your closet right now as still be perfectly happy. Why? Because everything that is going to be left in your closet is items which make you the happiest. Having a few, pieces of quality clothing which are going to last you several years is more than good enough to keep you happy.

Minimalism requires that you simplify your life and the things that you do. Eliminating the physical clutter from your life is a good place to start, but simplifying the things that you do extends to your social life, work schedule and all the other daily tasks which you usually find yourself occupied with. Take a look at your daily task list and ask yourself, is everything that is on this list right now important or urgent? How is completing this task going to benefit or impact me? If there is no significant benefit to be had, then perhaps the task is not as urgent as you think it might be. Simplify the clutter that is in your schedule by listing your commitments down, and then picking a few of the most important ones to get done in a day. Avoid over-cluttering and scheduling and scheduling commitments to yourself back to back, you need some breathing space and time for yourself in between for - that's right - the important things.

Simplifying your schedule is probably going to be as challenging as decluttering the physical items around your home. Many people find it hard to say "no" or to have to refuse an appointment or a social event for fear of disappointing others. Learning to say no is one of the hardest things to do, but it is important to remember that you cannot please everyone at the expense of forgoing your own happiness. If an appointment or a task is not important, and it is going to take up too much time away from what you should be focusing on, it's time to learn how to say no.

Cut back on your to-do list, because you don't need to do every single thing on the list. You only have a set number of hours in a day, and you don't want to spend all that time filling it with meaningless tasks which don't bring you happiness. A to-do list is going to be never-ending, and the only way it is going to be simplified is if you do something about it. Another common misconception that many walks around with is the notion that we need to be "busy" all the time. Being busy and being effective are two completely different things. Minimalists could have 5 items on their to-do list, but every single item is important and will produce the highest impact on their lives. Those 5 items meaningful items are going to be a lot more effective than having 10 items which produce little to no impact. Get the important stuff done first. Everything else can wait.

Minimalism's Little Rules

Okay, so there may not be any hard and fast rules when it comes to living your life as a minimalist, but there are some rules that minimalists could go to if they need a little guidance when it comes to decluttering.

- **The 20/20 Rule** - The first rule is going to eliminate the need for you to hold onto things under the "just in case I might need them" train of thought. How many times have you found it hard to get rid of old items in the past just because you were worried you might need them someday? The idea that you might need to hold onto your stuff in case there is ever a need in the far-off, hypothetical future where you may need it is how you end up with too much clutter. When you do hold onto those items, have you ever needed them up to this point? Be honest with yourself. Rarely do we end up using our "just in case" items and they end up doing nothing more than taking up space in your home. It's time to do away with these items, and the 20/20 rule is where you begin. Start by getting rid of all the "just in case" items which are under $20 dollars that you could easily replace in under 20 minutes. That way, if you ever find yourself in a predicament where you need one of these "just in case" items, you can easily replace them for under $20 dollars in under $20 minutes. Odds are that you won't miss or ever need all the "just in case" items you have been holding onto, and you won't need to replace them at all. Plus, your home is decluttered as an added benefit.
- **The 90/90 Rule** - Rules may be restrictive, but there are certain occasions where they may come in handy. The 90/90 rule is one of them. When attempting to simplify your life, you may sometimes find yourself stuck even before you've had a chance to properly start, particularly when you're being faced with a whole pile of your belongings which you need to start sorting through. When we find ourselves face to face with all your possessions, suddenly determining which items are valuable and which are not becomes almost impossible. Letting go then, becomes a nearly impossible task, because how do you decide what you should get rid of and what you should keep? Enter the 90/90 rule. Take a good look at everything that you own, and then pick something. Anything will do, doesn't matter what it is, as long as you pick something. Once you have your item, ask yourself if you have used this anytime within the last 90 days. If the answer is no, then ask yourself if you are going to use it within the next 90 days. If the answer is still no, then it's time to let it go. The 90/90 day rule is

just there to serve as a guideline, and you don't necessarily have to follow those numbers if they don't work for you. It could be a 60/60 day rule, maybe even a 120/120 day rule. Pick a number that works best for you.

- **The 10/10 Rule -** Think about everything that you own right now and ask yourself one very important question. How important is this stuff to you? Those material possessions which you worked so hard for, spent your hard earned money on, scrimped and saved to finally purchase, how much value does it really add to your life? Would you be surprised to find out that it matters less than you think? You might be with the 10/10 materialism rule. Here's how it works, take a pen and paper and write down the 10 most expensive items that you own within the last decade (10 years). This could be your car, laptop, mobile phone, any jewelry that was purchased, maybe even your home. List the 10 most expensive big-ticket purchases you made in the last 10 years. Grab another piece of paper and make a new list, this time with the 10 things which add the most value and meaning into your life. This list could include experiences like spending time with your loved ones on a vacation, or watching your kid's dance recital, maybe even having a lovely meal and catch up session with your parents. When you compare your list, it is likely that these two lists are going to have absolutely nothing in common. Now, ask yourself, which list brings you the greatest amount of happiness? You may just be surprised by your answer.

CHAPTER 3
Reality Check

As aesthetically pleasing as minimalism can be, especially around the home, the concept goes far beyond that. Being visual creatures, we tend to focus on what is in front of us since our perception is primarily rooted based on sight. What we consistently see in front set influences our state of emotions, it only stands to reason that the less mess and clutter you are surrounded with, the less stress you're likely to feel.

It is what helps to shape, condition and develop our mindset. It isn't just about learning to live with less so you can tell people that you are a minimalist. By embracing this approach, you are standing up against consumerism and rejecting the notion that our happiness is rooted only in material things. It is about learning how to be grateful, remain grounded, and learning how to be content and appreciative of everything that you have. It is only when you fully embrace minimalism that it dawns on you that you really don't need more stuff in your life at all. That the messages we have been exposed to all along have been wrong. We don't need one more thing to be happy, and there's no such thing as when I buy this then I will be happy because it doesn't exist because no matter how many things you buy it will never be enough. The only thing that is a guarantee is how stressed out you are going to be when you observed all the clutter of unnecessary and barely touched items around your home, wondering why you bought them in the first place.

Managing Your Expectations

You're ready to be done with your messy home, and you're ready to jump into minimalism, excited for the changes that it is about to bring into your life. Before you do though, there is something called the expectation gap that must be managed. This gap is what separates you from where you are right now, to where you would like to be in the future.

Let's say for example that you aim to be thriving as a minimalist within the next 3-months. Having high ambitions and goals is great, but the expectations that come with achieving that target will be accompanied by feelings of stress and anxiety from the pressure of wanting to achieve your target as soon as possible. Being focused far too much on the outcome will cause you to lose sight of being focused on the journey instead. Instead of having enjoyed the process of your journey towards becoming a minimalist, you're not having fun and all, and somewhere along the way, you'll begin to question why you wanted to initiate this change in the first place because this is not what you expected.

Expectations can act as a shackle that makes life more difficult than it should, or needs to be. There's nothing wrong with having standards and expectations, not at all. In fact, they give you something to work towards and to strive for. However, there is a very critical difference between standards and expectations. By its very definition, expectations are the beliefs we hold that certain events or outcomes are going to happen, and these expectations are based on strong assumptions that we hold about what the future might look like.

Imagine this scenario for a minute. Your husband or wife has had a long day at work. You want to do something nice for them to brighten up their day, and you decide to prepare a wonderful surprise dinner for them. You've done the grocery shopping, cooked their favorite foods, set the table and everything is primed and ready for their return. When your spouse returns, however, they will immediately walk into the house and say how they've had a horrible day and they're not feeling very hungry so they're going to go take a bath to try and relax. Your immediate reaction might be to feel anger or disappointment. After all that effort you put into it, they're not even appreciative, happy or excited the way that you expected them to be. But it isn't your spouse's fault that they failed to live up to your expectations, because these were your expectations, and no one, not even your spouse, is obligated to fulfill any of them.

That example illustrates why there is a need for us to manage our expectations. If possible, these expectations should be avoided altogether, as it can cause a great deal of grief if they are not met. You are bound to have had similar experiences in the past, where you've been let down and disappointed because things didn't go the way you thought it would, not realizing that expectations were the reason behind the emotions that you felt.

Before you begin your new venture into minimalism, you need to manage your expectations to avoid being disappointed if you find it wasn't all that you expected it to be. An expectation, when you get right down to it, is nothing more than your "best guess" about a possible outcome which you think might happen. These best guesses are made up of nothing more than your opinions and your hope. Once you realize that, you can begin working on keeping those unrealistic expectations at bay by:

- **Never Making Assumptions** - If you don't know a definitive answer to something, always ask and never assume. Assumptions are merely another way of "guessing" what's going to happen, and you will save yourself a lot of time, energy and disappointed by forgoing it.
- **Taking It One Day At a Time** - You never know what the day is going to bring. You could plan out your schedule to the minute, but unexpected situations will happen every now and then and these are beyond your control. Learning how to take it one day at a time is how you prevent yourself from feeling disappointed if things don't go according to plan.
- **Know the Difference Between Goals and Expectations** - Your goals are concrete and fact-based, whereas expectations are

based upon your opinions and hopes. A goal is something tangible that you can work towards.
- **Be Realistic About the Outcome** - Expecting something to be easy is where the trouble begins. If you begin your journey towards minimalism expecting things to be as simple as clearing out the excess stuff in your home and you're done, you're going to find yourself challenged every step of the way when you start realizing that it is not that simple and there's a lot more involved in the process.
- **Preparing for Possible Problems** - There are bound to be challenges along the way, even more so when something involves a major life change like switching to minimalism. Anticipating the possible problems along the way which might come up is how you prepare yourself and save yourself from feeling discouraged or disappointed.
- **Being Adaptable** - It is easy to feel emotional when things don't go the way you planned, but that's what reality is. Things will change, and situations will shift all the time, sometimes in the moments when you least expect it. Sometimes they're good changes, and sometimes they aren't, but the more adaptable and open you are to these changes, the better you'll be able to manage what comes your way. Challenges never last forever, and just because of the unexpected happened, it doesn't mean you failed at achieving your goal.

Keep your expectations low, but let your standards remain high. Having high standards is not about achieving perfectionism, but rather it is the determination and commitment you are making to yourself not to take shortcuts or to cut corners. High standards it the commitment that you make to yourself to always put your best effort into everything that you do.

The Myths and Misconceptions

Possibly the reason for a lot of the confusion and misconception is that minimalism is such a unique concept that is unlike anything we have become accustomed to growing up. It is an extremely personal journey, and since everyone is different, it stands to reason that it is always going to be approached and practiced differently based on the preferences of the individual. What one person may view as valuable, another might not, which is why you'll never find two minimalists with the exact same setup in their homes.

Minimalism is a concept as diverse as the people who practice it. People of all ages, races, genders, religions, and nationalities are practitioners of this movement which just continues to grow as more people are becoming aware that true happiness and freedom lies in letting go of their attachment to their worldly possessions. Yet, this concept continues to be misunderstood by a large percentage of people, surrounded by myths and misconceptions that cause confusion and hesitation.

Myth: Success Is Defined By How Much We Earn

Zig Ziglar said it best when he said: "money will not make you happy, but this is something everyone wants to discover for themselves". Changing the mindset that has been around for a long time is not going to happen overnight, but minimalists are slowly working towards making that change in their lives, and that's a good place to start.

Myth: Being a Minimalist Is Only About Reducing How Much Stuff You Own

It is also about your expectations, and as we have learned, keeping your expectations low is how you remain focused on the journey, not the destination. Minimalism is not just about how much stuff you own, it is the pathway to a life of content in every aspect that extends far beyond materialism.

Myth: My Home Is Going to Be All Stark, Boring, and Barren

Only if you want it to be. Your home is your own, and what stays or goes is entirely up to you. Minimalism simply encourages you to keep the meaningful things around while discarding everything else that is unnecessary and no longer serves a purpose in your life. A minimalist home can still have decoratives and bright colorful patterns that brighten up space if you want it to. A minimalist home can still have beautiful paintings or pictures of your family and friends on the wall if you want them. Actually, the only real difference between the home of a minimalist and everyone else is the absence of clutter and junk. Minimalists still decorate their homes, but they do it with simplicity. They still have several pieces of furniture around, but only what they need to live comfortably and nothing more. Your home is your own, and you can keep or discard anything you like as long as you're happy about it.

Myth: Being a Minimalist Means No More Fun

Again, only if you decide on it, minimalism isn't restrictive in any way, and what you do or don't do is entirely up to you. In fact, minimalism could actually help you carve out more time for fun and excitement in your life by helping you declutter your schedule and only keep the tasks which are important. All the other mundane tasks which take up too much of your time with no real benefit are the ones which are robbing you of the fun you could be having while doing something that you loved instead.

Myth: Being a Minimalist Means I Can't Own Nice Things

Would it surprise you to learn that you could own even nicer things than what you had before by being a minimalist? When you no longer spend on the unnecessary, you're left with a lot more room in your budget to spend on quality necessities instead. Owning fewer things doesn't mean you don't anything nice, and many minimalists are doing quite the opposite. Investing in quality items when there is a need for them means minimalists actually own much nicer things when they're not focused on only purchasing cheaper products while compromising on quality.

Myth: You Are Only Allowed Once of Each Item

Having fewer possessions doesn't necessarily mean you only have one of each item. The whole having only one of each approach is only going to work for the items which make sense. Having just one bookshelf or one television makes sense, but having just one spoon, fork or plate is not going to make sense, especially if you have other people living in your home. It is safe to say that this one is an absolute myth and completely untrue. Minimalism has no rules or limits, and you should have multiples of some items if it is the sensible and logical thing to do.

Myth: Minimalism Means You Can't Live In A Big Home

Living in a smaller home doesn't make you any more of a minimalist if your home is still full of clutter. The size of your home is not what matters at the end of the day, it is what your home is filled with. If you have a family of four or five, it wouldn't make sense for you to squeeze everyone into a one bedroom unit just so you could call yourself a minimalist. Being unhappy and uncomfortable is not what this concept is about, not at all. You can live in a big house that is suitable for the size of your family and still be just as much of a minimalist as someone who is living in a considerably smaller abode.

Myth: Minimalism Is Just Material

The material aspect of it all is what most people tend to focus on because that's the immediate thing which springs to mind when you mention the word "minimalism". Say the word to someone who is unfamiliar with the concept and they're likely to think "it means I have to get rid of all my stuff". Those who practice minimalism, however, knows that the main takeaway lesson here is about reducing the chaos and clutter in your life, and this can come from anywhere. It could be your busy, packed schedule that is causing you chaos and is in need of minimalism. It could be your emotional or spiritual side which you have lost touch with because of all the distractions that your life is filled with. Perhaps that is in need of some minimalism. Or it could be any one of the relationships in your life that are weighing you down which might benefit from some minimalism. The material aspect of it all is just one, the small portion that makes up the overall concept of what minimalism is all about.

Myth: Everything in Your Home Needs To Be White

Only if white happens to be your favorite color. Sure, the pictures we see of minimalists homes do look rather impressive with their one-tone color scheme, but if it doesn't work for you, there's no reason you need to follow along. Fill your home with as many colors as you like if it makes you happy to do it. Your home is your sanctuary, your happy place, and it should be filled with any color scheme you like.

Myth: You Need to Either Be Only a Minimalist, Or Have Kids, But You Can't Do Both

Why not do both? True, maintaining a clean and clutter-free environment may seem like an almost impossible task with kids around, but that doesn't mean that minimalists refrain from having kids altogether. Or that they have to choose only one approach to go with. You can be a minimalist and be a parent at the same time, and in fact, this could provide a wonderful learning opportunity to teach your kids about the valuable things in life from a young age. Kids don't need dozens of toys or electronics to be happy when they can get that same amount of happiness or more by spending quality time together as a family building experiences and memories instead.

Misconception: Minimalists Are Lazy People

Minimalism is unique to the individual who practices it. There are some who may be lazy it is true, but that doesn't mean that all minimalists are like that. Living a simpler life doesn't mean you're automatically lazy. The notion that we have to be "busy" all the time to be considered productive is one of the biggest misconceptions around. There are hardworking people and there are lazy people, but minimalism is not a determining factor. If someone is lazy from the start, that is simply who they are and it has nothing to do with minimalism.

Misconception: Minimalists Are Extreme When It Comes To The Environment

Minimalism cares about the environment, but that doesn't mean you have to go to extreme lengths for it. Minimalists simply do their part for the environment by making a conscious effort to consume and discard fewer resources, but again, this would entirely depend on the individual. Different people will have a different approach to the way that they live their lives, and not everyone who embraces the life of a minimalist is going to go to extreme measures just to feel satisfied knowing that they have done their part.

Misconception: Minimalists Need to Be Vegans or Vegetarians

You don't have to be, but if you want to for your own reasons, you could be. Not all minimalists are vegans or vegetarians. Once again, a completely personal choice that is entirely up to you.

Misconception: Minimalists Are People Who Are Young, Single and Free

You can embrace minimalism at any stage of your life. Young, single, old or married, it doesn't matter since there are no age restrictions with this approach to living. A lot of minimalists actually embraced this lifestyle at an older age when they want a clean slate or to start over because they may not necessarily be happy with the direction their life has taken. No matter what your reasons may be or why you decided to get started, minimalism has no age limit and you can do this at any stage in your life. Even kids can do it if you show them how to.

Misconception: Minimalists Don't Keep Books Around

It's not that they avoid keeping or holding onto books entire, but rather they make a selective choice about the books that they keep around. It's all about keeping it simple and only keeping what's important. The Kindle has also made it less necessary to keep physical copies of books around the home when you can easily store everything you need on one digital device, saving you tons of space in the process.

Misconception: Minimalists Are Constantly Counting and Keeping Track of Their Possessions

Some minimalists may do it, others may not. Minimalism is all about preference and personal choice. What one minimalist does, another might not. There's no rule that says everyone has to live in the exact same way. If it makes someone happy to count their possessions and limit the number of things they allow themselves to own, they are free to do just that. There is no magic number, only a number that works for you. If it makes you happy to only own 50 items, go ahead and do it. If it makes you happy to own 100 items, why not?

Misconception: Minimalists Aren't Sentimental People

You don't need to keep boxes upon boxes of sentimental items to be considered someone who is sentimental. Minimalists are sentimental too, they just do it a little differently by finding value and only holding onto the things which they consider to be the truly important pieces of significance to them. You'd be surprised to know that a lot of minimalists actually choose to display their most sentimental items somewhere around their now clutter-free home because they have the space for it. Instead of being tucked away in a box gathering dust and being forgotten, displaying them around the home serves as a reminder for them about what they value the most.

Misconception: Minimalists Can Be Rather Pompous and Condescending

Some people just naturally have that kind of personality, but it is in no way a reflection of how other minimalists are. Everyone is a unique individual in their own right. There could be some minimalists who love the way that they live and want to share that with everyone that they know but is perhaps going about it in the wrong way which is why they come off as pompous and condescending. That might not be their intention at all, having some individuals like that doesn't make all minimalists automatically pompous or condescending.

Misconception: Minimalists Avoid Spending Money

Only because this makes sense, why would you continuously waste money on unnecessary items that you don't need and most like will not end up using at all? Those funds could be directed towards better use, such as saving for retirement, putting it into your kids' college fund, or saving for a rainy day. It's not that minimalists avoid spending money altogether, but rather they exercise precaution over the things that they do spend on. Minimalism doesn't restrict or stop you from spending money, it simply reminds you to stop and think before you part with your hard-earned cash by asking yourself if you really need it. Minimalists are also wiser with their spending, choosing quality over quantity. Plus, they have come to understand that spending money doesn't equate to happiness.

Misconception: Minimalists Cant' Have Any Collections
If your collections make you happy and add meaning to your life, you're more than welcome to hold onto them. Keep the collections that hold valuable meaning for you, and balance that out by getting rid of the items that don't hold quite as much value and wouldn't be missed. Some collections are worth holding onto, and it is up to you to decide what stays and what goes. Having a passion which involves collectibles doesn't mean you're not a minimalist.

CHAPTER 4
Getting Started

Alright, so we have come to the part where it's finally time to get started on becoming a minimalist. All those pictures of beautiful, clutter-free, visually appealing homes you've been enviously eyeing on the Internet, that's about to be what your home now looks like. Not exactly the same of course, but close enough.

People still tend to underestimate how distracting clutter can be. It is a form of visual distraction, and just because it doesn't seem like you're thinking much about it, somewhere in your brain it still bothers you. Every visual thing that we encounter tugs on our attention, even if it is just a little. Have you ever wondered why a minimalist home seems to have that calming effect whenever you look at it? Or even when you walk into one? That's because there's not a lot going on there that is distracting you.

Not to mention how easy it is going to be from now on to clean your home when you don't have a whole bunch of stuff that you constantly need to dust, or piles of stuff on the floor making it hard for you to sweep and vacuum. The more you have, the more time you spend cleaning, it really is that simple, and you're going to now save yourself so much time that you're going to wonder why you didn't start adopting this approach years ago.

Minimalists work hard to keep their home neat and free of clutter because they don't want anything in their home that is weighing them down, stressing them out or wasting their time. A minimalist is content with the things that they already have because they have managed to make the shift in their mindset from I need to acquire to I already have more than enough. The clutter in your home is a reflection on who you are. For example, you're holding onto things longer than you should, even when it no longer serves a purpose because you're afraid to let go of the past. You constantly keep buying because you may be operating based on the fear mentality, and you would rather than unnecessary items stored away just in case rather because you believe it is better to be with them than without them. Maybe the clutter that is piling up in your home which you never seem to have time to clean is a reflection of your too-busy schedule.

What Can I Expect My Minimalist Home to Look Like?

That depends on course on the kind of home you have, what your personal decorative tastes are and just how extreme you plan to go with the decluttering process. The pictures you see on the Internet are some examples of what your home could look like, but that doesn't necessarily mean that's how your home should look like. Think of them as inspirations instead to give you an idea of where to begin. However, there are some basic characteristics which are standard in the home of a minimalist:

- **The Furniture** - Your furniture is going to be cut down to only the very few essential pieces that you are going to need and nothing more. The furniture would depend on the room it's in. The bedroom, for instance, might only require a simple bed, a dresser, and a nightstand as the few basic staple pieces of furniture. Depending on your tastes, space, and needs, you could choose to have a rug, perhaps a bookshelf or even a small couch by the window if that is where you like to sit and relax. The room should only have what is needed, nothing more.
- **The Surfaces** - The thing you will immediately notice about minimalist homes is how much free space is available when it's not being littered or cluttered with piles of stuff. Most minimalists will aim to keep the flat surfaces of their home neat, clean and free, save for a few pieces of decorative items here and there. There will definitely be no stacks of papers piling up, or piles of books and papers, or things thrown about in a haphazard manner.
- **The Decorations** - Minimalists choose accent decorations which care carefully chosen and selectively placed around their home, and it is usually done to spice up the place a little. Instead of having a completely empty coffee table surface, there might be a simple vase with some flowers placed as an accent decoration. Minimalists like being clutter free, but they're not that extreme.
- **Clearing the Kitchen** - The best place to start in the kitchen would be by clearing the sink of any dirty dishes before tackling the other parts. Spend a good 10-15 minutes clearing and scrubbing the dishes, and cleaning the sink area and the surrounding areas. Once you're done, step back and take a few minutes to admire how clean it now looks, then take that motivation and bring it with you as you begin scrubbing and clearing away the other parts of your kitchen. Anything that is expired in the fridge and pantry needs to go immediately.
- **Separating Into Piles** - This one works especially well for clothing. Separate your items into piles of either Keep, Maybe and Toss or into piles based on how often you use these items, which could be Frequently, Occasionally and Never. Put everything that you're unsure of in a separate pile that you can come back later and revisit, so you don't spend too much time sorting through your items. Although it is important to think carefully about each item, you don't want to spend too long making a decision because you need to keep the process moving. Otherwise decluttering would take forever.

Beginning the Decluttering Process

This is going to be a massive project. Deciding what to get rid of would be the first part of your decluttering challenge. The second is the actual decluttering process. Looking around at everything you have to do, you might start to feel overwhelmed at the immense workload that's waiting for you (depending on the size of your home and how much stuff you have). Where do you even begin and how long is this going to take? Try and relax, take a breath and use the following guide to help you work through the process one step at a time:

- **Working in Sections** - You don't need to do your entire home all at once, this is going to be almost impossible to do unless you're living alone, without much belongings and in a very small place of your own. There's no need to rush through the process, so don't put any pressure on yourself trying to finish everything in a day. Take your time working through each room, focusing on the task of decluttering and carefully considering which items should stay and which should go. You might end up getting rid of something you didn't mean to if you were to hurry through everything, take your time, and do it one room at a time.
- **Checking Out the Furniture** - The furniture is usually going to be the biggest items that you own, taking up the most space in your room. Start the simplifying process by checking out your furniture and determining which items can be donated or relocated to a different part of the house where they might be more beneficial. Remember to only keep what you need, and the fewer pieces of furniture you have, the better, but keep it within reason of course. Eliminate your furniture without sacrificing your comfort and happiness.
- **Start With the Flat Surfaces** - Once you've finished sorting out the furniture, look at all the other flat surfaces around your home and start working on clearing those one surface at a time. Pick a countertop, a table, perhaps even a part some shelves that need clearing away. Once you've finished with one flat surface, move onto the next. Again, this doesn't have to be done all at once, take as much time as you need and work methodically through the process.
- **Clearing the Floors** - Except for furniture, there is nothing else which should be touching the ground and blocking your pathway. The floor should be completely clear of everything except furniture, no piles, no boxes, and no stacks of items. Once you have removed most of the furniture except the essentials, clear everything else that may be lying on the floor. Either find a different home of it, donate it or toss it in the trash if it can't be donated.

- **Out of Sight** - Everything in the home of a minimalist as a "home" of its own. The books have a home (bookshelf). The stationary has a home (desk drawers). The artwork has a home (hanging on the walls). The clothes have a home (closet). Nothing is cluttering and left out in the open because everything has been neatly stored away out of sight until it is needed. A minimalist always knows just where to find everything that they need in their home because it is organized and kept where it should be.

With every stage of the decluttering process, you need to look at each item you're about to remove carefully and ask yourself if this is essential. Furniture, clothing, books, even stationary and decorative items. Everything. If you can live without it, then you can get rid of it. The main goal now is to just strip each room in your home down to the bare essentials which you need for survival. Everything else may be added later on if it becomes a necessity.

Decluttering Your Workspace

An uncluttered workspace is a beautiful thing to look at. Those beautiful pictures online just inspire you to sit down and work for hours because of how peaceful it looks, with the bright sunlight streaming through the windows and nothing but a laptop and a coffee mug on your desk. Which makes you reflect on what your current workspace looks like right now.

Much like your home, the workspace of a minimalist is going to be different based on the individual. Some people might like the more extreme approach where the only thing that sits on their desk is a laptop and nothing else. Others might like to have one or two accented decorative items on the desk, along with the computer to help add more of an aesthetic appeal that they like to look at.

When you think about decluttering your workspace, whether at home or at the office, think about the items which are most essential to you - the items that you used throughout the day. The workspace that you set up for yourself should have all the minimum requirements that you need to function effectively and productively. If what you need to function productively on top of your desk is a laptop, a notepad and a pen to scribble ideas, have only those items on top of your desk and tuck everything else away.

As for organizing the rest of your items, you want to think about simplifying and streamlining the workflow process to make it as efficient as possible for yourself. If your desk comes with drawers, the first drawer should be arranged according to what you need to function most effectively, the second drawer with what you don't need as frequently and so on. In short, arrange your drawers by order of importance. Anything else that is not essential to your workflow can be removed.

Even your laptop or computer can be decluttered and kept simple. Some minimalists even have just a desktop with no folders on it at all. Again, the setup that you choose for yourself needs to be based on what you need

to work. Here are a couple of tips to help you declutter and streamline your productivity:
- **Downsizing Your Inbox** - Do you have multiple emails that you use? Streamline that by downsizing to just one email and one inbox for all your needs. That one inbox rule extends to beyond your computer too, if having papers is unavoidable in your line of work. Limit it to just one inbox tray for all your papers, including the sticky post-it notes and reminders. This is useful at work, and if you have colleagues who are in the habit of dropping documents on your desk when you're not around, have a conversation with them and ask if they would be so kind as to put the papers on the inbox tray on your desk instead. Make it a point to clear your inbox regularly, both your emails and the inbox tray on your desk. Create folders in your emails to sort them so there's nothing on your main page except for the new emails that come in each day. If you no longer need the email, delete it. As for the inbox tray on your desk, clear it as often as possible, either weekly or daily if you can manage it. Anything that you don't need to hold onto to can be trashed.
- **Clear Flat Surface** - The same rules apply to your work desk as they do to the other flat surfaces in your home. Keep it neat, clean and clutter free except for one of two items. Unless you're actively working on some papers or documents, there should be none of these on your desk at any time. Post-it notes should be tucked away in your drawers until you need them, along with any pens, stapler or other basic stationary which you use regularly. Clear away as much as you can and leave nothing on your desk but a laptop and maybe one or two accented decorations again. No, knick-knacks, not trinkets, not even little souvenirs from colleagues should be displayed on your desk. Anything that is unnecessary and not contributing to your work routine needs to go.
- **Nothing On the Walls** - Is your home office wall cluttered with all kinds of stuff posted on it? Well, the walls are going to have to be stripped bare too. Like the rest of your home, there should be nothing on the walls except for one or two pieces of decorative artwork for ambiance. At work, clear your cubicle walls of any visual clutter that should not be there. Everything should be stripped bare so there's no distraction happening. Since you don't have four walls to work with here, if you need to have a motivational image or two for inspiration, downsize the image according to your cubicle measurements so it doesn't take up too much space.
- **A Simple Filing System Is All Your Need** - Is there even a need to keep physical paper copies anymore when everything is

easily stored online in the cloud? If you simply must have a hard copy of certain documents, simplify your filing process by only limiting it to one copy per document. You don't need multiple copies of each anymore, and if you're worried about losing the digital copies of these documents which you might be keeping on your computer, back them up online and have a copy in the digital space instead of the physical one. At least there's no visual clutter to look at, and it's a much better approach than filing where you still run the risk of losing the documents should you misplace the file.

I'm Afraid to Let Things Go

That's perfectly understandable. You have probably spent most of your entire life up to this point being surrounded by belongings that you don't know any other way or how you would survive without them. The inability to let things go is the fear mentality, and you worry about parting with your items because of all the questions that raise fear within you at the very thought of it. What if I need it again? This has an emotional connection to me, how can I let it go? What if I'm giving away something that I might later regret? What if I need it next time and I can't buy it anymore?

You may think it is wasteful to get rid of your things, especially when they're still in good condition, but so is holding onto them when they are going to serve you no purpose. If you don't love them anyway, why hold onto them when you know you might never use them? It is wasting valuable space in your home. It is wasting your time when you have to spend several extra minutes tidying up or keeping them clean. It is a waste of resources to hold onto them when you could donate them to someone who might need it more than you do.

If something holds a sentimental value to you, but you know it's never going to be used, take a picture of these items for you to keep before you donate them. The reason you have an emotional attachment to them is not because of what they can do for you or how they can be used, it's because of the memories they might hold. Taking a picture of them is a way for you to find balance, where you still get to hold onto these items in a way, while still donating them to someone with a greater need. You still have the memories with you, but they now take up no space in your home.

For the items that you genuinely can't bring yourself to give away because it would upset you far too much, start a separate storage box for them. This way there aren't just strewn about the home randomly and neatly organized instead.

What To Do With the Stuff You Don't Need?

If you're wondering what to do with all of the items that are tossed in the trash, there are several options which you could consider:

- Having a yard sale where interested neighbors can come and pick out which items of yours they would like.
- Donating them to charity organizations like Goodwill.
- Selling your items on eBay.
- Donating them to friends or family who might be interested or have a use for them.
- Sell your used books online or consider donating them to the library if they are still in excellent condition.
- Recycling your stuff.
- If there are unused items which are brand new and recently bought but you've changed your mind about them, consider giving them away as gifts instead.

Setting Goals and Making Plans

New habits can be a challenge to form and keep. Even harder when you don't have a goal which gives you something to work towards. Yes, minimalism is a habit that must be formed. You're about to completely change the way that you live as you know it, and as excited as you are to begin this journey, it is still going to take some time to get used to it. All change comes with its own challenges. Have you ever tried to form a new habit without having a proper goal set out for yourself? You're excited and pumped up, ready to get going, but along the way, you lose that motivational spark that got you started, and you end up giving up midway through the process. It happens more often than you think.

It is easy to try and implement a new habit in the beginning during the first few weeks, only to have that initial excite wane as you progress over the next few days or weeks. It's sometimes hard to make a new habit stick, even with the best intentions. Busy schedules, hectic lives, tiredness, temptation, and even emotions tend to get in the away and side sweep us. This is why diet fads never last long, and weight loss intentions come and go. We lose interest in the initial novelty of it all and despite what we hope for, we find ourselves slipping back into our old routine and way of life before we know it.

Since we don't want that to happen with your intention to become a minimalist, it is important to set goals and make plans for yourself to help you stick to this routine until it becomes a lifelong habit. As you begin this process, lay out all the goals that you have for yourself. Write them down, and then look again at the list you have just written. If you've got more than two or three goals written on there, you need to break it down and work on it in stages. Just like decluttering your home.

Trying to do too much too soon is a common downfall of many good intentions. Just like clearing out your home, if you try to tackle everything all at once, you're only going to end up feeling overwhelmed and stressed out by the whole process. It is okay to take your time working through your goals too. Slow and steady wins the race at the end of the day. Pick out one goal to start with if that is easier for you to manage, but have no more than three goals at a time which you're working on. Pick out one goal and tell yourself that you're going to spend the next 30-days committing to making this goal a reality.

That's all you need to do. One goal, 30-days. If you manage to accomplish that goal before the end of that 30-days, move onto the next goal. No fuss, no frills, no stress, just one goal at a time. By simply making this one tweak alone to the process, you're relieving yourself of an immense amount of pressure you might otherwise feel when you're rushing to keep up with your goals. Always remind yourself that there is no urgency, and whenever you find yourself feeling pressed, stop and ask yourself what's the rush? Having only one goal to work on at a time allows yourself to devote your full attention, focus and commit to what you're doing. It also allows you time to enjoy the process rather than simply going through the motions for the sake of doing so. When you mindfully focus on what you're doing, you're aware why you're doing it and how it is benefitting you, which keeps you motivated to move forward.

CHAPTER 5
Financial Freedom Through Minimalism

It's been established by now that minimalism isn't just about clearing out the stuff in your home. It involves several other areas of your life too, like your finances for example. Minimalists still spend money, they just spend their money differently. How have they managed to do that? By not making money or material possessions the primary focus of their life anymore.

Now that you have decluttered most of your home and your closet, it's time to tackle the nation material objects, starting with your finances. You're going to be amazed by how much clarity being smart with your money and having a minimalist budget is going to be. There is one caveat that needs to be mentioned, however, and that is simplifying your finances doesn't necessarily mean you'll be spending significantly less money. Minimalism teaches you to focus on quality over quantity, and quality items don't always come with an affordable price tag. You'll be spending less frequently, but not necessarily on less expensive items, and therein lies the difference between minimalism and living frugally.

Minimalism vs. Frugal Living

Yes, minimalism and frugality are two very different concepts. One is focused on owning fewer items, while the latter is focused on spending less on items.

Living frugally teaches its followers to get on getting the most out of their money by being thrifty. Using coupons at the supermarket, scouring the internet or catalogs for the best sales and deals. Trying to find the cheapest possible option, that's what being frugal is. Frugal people can still own a significant amount of possessions because they're not focused on decluttering, they're focused on stretching their dollars to the limit. A frugal person will take $50 and get three new pairs of shoes which are of average quality but cheap, while a minimalist will take that same $50 and just get one pair of quality shoes that will last a long time. Since they're not focused on owning fewer times, living frugally can lead to the accumulation of clutter over time.

A frugal person will:
- Never purchase items at full price
- Do most of their shopping at thrift or discount stores
- Look for the best deals they can get before spending their money
- Live below their means to save money
- Use coupons if it means even greater savings
- Be willing to buy second-hand, depending on the item and the quality
- Do their buying in bulk from wholesale stores for even bigger savings

A minimalist will:
- Get rid of all the unused items in their home
- Donate the clothes that they have not worn in over a year
- Say no to buying the things that they know they don't need
- Be willing to spend money on experiences instead of items
- Have no emotional attachment to the items they own
- Work on simplifying every area of their life
- Set goals and priorities which help them live intentionally
- Focus on prioritizing quality over quantity

Minimalism and frugality are different, but they're not exclusive. If you're wondering whether it's possible to be both a minimalist and be frugal, the answer is yes. In fact, being both makes you a powerhouse. As a frugal person, you want to spend less on what you intend to buy, and at the same time as a minimalist, you're only planning to buy what you need. Being both means you still care about quality, but you're not willing to overpay for it because you care about how your hard earned dollars are being spent.

How Minimalism Is Going to Transform Your Finances

It is amazing what simplifying your financial life can do for you. Taking responsibility and taking control of your spending is bringing you one step closer to financial freedom. Instead of constantly struggling every month to stay on top of your spending and your bills, you are not going to take back control by being mindful about where your money is going.

Financial minimalism teaches you how to stop feeling overwhelmed and guilty about how and where you're spending your money by taking the first step towards owning your finances. To be accountable for your spending habits, a responsibility which will lead to making more informed choices about the decisions that you make in regards to your spending. There's going to be less of the "I don't know where my money went!", and more of the "I know EXACTLY where my money went."

Minimalism is going to help you transform your finances by:
- **Encouraging You to Prioritize** - Learning how to embrace and focus on only the things which matter to you is going to now be carried over into your spending habits. When you shift your focus to experiences rather than material possessions, it can be easier to determine what you want to buy and what you don't. If you know your priority is to save for a vacation with your family, you're not going to want to spend on getting a new t-shirt which you don't need, even if it is on sale. If you know your priority is to take your parents out to a nice dinner for their anniversary, you're going to redirect your resources towards that instead of spending on another pair of shoes you don't need.
- **Budgeting Based on Priorities** - Once you've got your priorities sorted out, the next step is to plan a workable budget

based on those priorities. This too becomes much easier when you know what's important to you, and setting a budget based on those priorities will set a clear direction as to how and where your money should be spent. Having a budget will also help you put your spending into perspective. Take a look at where your money is going right now. If those areas of spending are not in line with your new priorities as a minimalist, cut them out and redirect those funds towards your savings or paying off debt.

- **Increasing Your Savings** - All that money which was previously spent buying frivolous and unnecessary items can now be channeled and put to good use by saving it instead. Increasing your savings and putting more money aside than you could before will leave you with enough to put a little aside for a rainy day and pay off any debts you've got. Less shopping, more savings and debt paying, and one step closer to financial freedom when you're no longer weighed down by debt.
- **Fuelling Your Motivation** - When you start seeing how quickly your debt is reducing as pay it off with the money you now have leftover from not buying unnecessary stuff, you'll be motivated to keep going as the finish line to becoming debt free draws one step closer with each payment that you make. Getting rid of debt is one of the most liberating financial experiences because, without that burden, more doors and possibilities start to open. You can take that vacation with your family you've been wanting to for so long, or pursue your passion with the funds you now have to spare not having to pay off any debt. With no additional monthly payments and more money left over from unnecessary spending, you now have the freedom to explore the things that you love the most.
- **Starting An Emergency Fund** - Everyone should have an emergency fund just in case. These funds should be easily accessible (but not too easy to avoid temptation) and only to be used in an absolute emergency when you've exhausted all other options. As you free yourself from all the clutter that's taking up space in your life, see which items can be sold so that money can be used to help you give your finances the boost that it should have had years ago.

Financial Freedom Begins with Simplifying Your Finances

Cutting down and simplifying your finances begins with cutting out all the unnecessary expenditure. Common expenses that the average person would have every month include:
- Rent or mortgage payments
- Homeowner's insurance
- Utilities

- Car payments
- Gas bill
- Cable TV bill
- Internet bill
- Mobile bill
- Grocery shopping
- Miscellaneous shopping (new clothes, shoes, books, etc)
- Credit card (or cards depending on how many you have)
- Student loans
- Miscellaneous debt
- Gym membership
- Health insurance
- Medical expenses

Once you've got a list of your monthly expenses, assess which items can be eliminated so that list becomes simplified? Some expenses can't be helped of course, but for the ones which can be removed, ask yourself, "Do I really need this to make me happy?" Your priorities are going to help you cut back on a lot from the list above, and here's what a minimalist monthly expense might look like instead:

- Rent or mortgage payments
- Homeowners insurance
- Utilities
- ~~Car payment~~ (sell the car if not needed)
- ~~Gas bill~~ (no longer needed without a car)
- ~~Cable TV bill~~ (canceled subscription because you barely watch cable anyway, and Netflix has made it easier to enjoy your favorite shows online so all you need is the internet)
- Internet bill
- Mobile bill
- Grocery shopping
- ~~Miscellaneous shopping (new clothes, shoes, books, etc)~~ (don't need this anymore now that you're focused on accumulating less)
- ~~Credit card (or cards depending on how many you have)~~ (paid off from the money saved by spending less)
- ~~Student loans~~ (paid off from the money saved by spending less)
- ~~Miscellaneous debt~~ (paid off from the money saved by spending less)
- ~~Gym membership~~ (don't need this, exercising outdoors is just as good and free)
- Health insurance
- Medical expenses

That list has now become significantly shorter without all the unnecessary spending incurred:

- Rent or mortgage payments
- Homeowners insurance

- Utilities
- Internet bill
- Mobile bill
- Grocery shopping
- Health insurance
- Medical expenses

Of course, everyone's monthly expenses are going to look different based on lifestyle and needs, this example is just to illustrate how much you could be saving by simply cutting back on the things that you don't need. As you get more adjusted to living like a minimalist, you'll be able to reassess your budget and expenditure as you go along and make even more adjustments when you feel there are other areas which you no longer need. Minimalists find happiness in being content with what they have, and when you've already got everything that you need to be happy, you stop looking for more ways to spend your money.

The bottom line with debt is that to get out of it, you need to spend less than what you're making. Everyone can find ways to keep things simple, regardless of how much money you're making or what your monthly spending patterns are like. There is always some area that you can cut back on. Logically, it should be a simple enough concept to follow. Spend less, save more, yet many Americans are still knee deep in debt and relying on multiple credit cards just to get by. If your spending continues to exceed what you make each month, the only thing that is going to grow (besides your clutter) is your debt. Simplifying your finances means to take a realistic look at what you actually need to survive comfortably each month, versus what you think you need to be happy.

How to Get Started With Your Own Minimalist Budget

Tackling your finances can be just as overwhelming and stressful as decluttering the physical items in your home, but that doesn't mean it should be used as an excuse to hold you back. It will only hold you back if you allow it to.

Unlike what you might think, getting started with a minimalist budget actually begins with a change in your mindset, before you start jumping in right away into your finances. You can't begin your budget anew if you're still carrying around old habits and ways of thinking about money. Change your mindset first and foremost about borrowing or owing money, whether this is to a financial institution or someone that you know. It is common to hear many people talk about how they bought a new car because they got a really great deal or it, or because the monthly payments were really low and it was simply too good a deal to pass up. These people are trying to stretch out their finances as much as they possibly can by trying to secure the lowest monthly payments. They do it because they believe that this is going to make them happy living beyond their means in a lifestyle which - if they're being honest - can't really afford, but feel entitled to.

Becoming a minimalist is going to require you to flip this kind of thinking on its head. Minimalists need to think along the lines of ownership, instead of what the lowest monthly payments are. Don't ask how much it is going to cost you every month, ask instead - what is the outright cost of buying the item? This isn't just limited to new car purchases, but any big-ticket items that you're going to pay for in installments (owing money). When you limit your available payment options, like your credit cards, it will make you stop and consider if you really can afford this item you're about to spend money on, more importantly, whether you need it.

To change your mindset, you need to establish a very clear set of financial values to help you out. Examples of these values could include living a life that is debt free, or saving at least 20% of your monthly income, or even to have at least a 30% buffer separating your income and your expenses. Having a clear set of financial values will help you then work on your priorities and finally, set your financial goals, which will help get you from where you are right now to where you want to be.

Examples of what your financial priorities might look like based upon the values you set above include making it a priority to pay off as much of your debt within the next 2 to 3 years and then using that money to channel it towards increasing that 20% savings you initially targeted. Or it could be to increase your income by another 20% so there's an even greater buffer percentage between your income and your expenses. From there, your goals could be to have at least $10,000 in your savings account by the end of the year or to have at least one credit card paid off and canceled by the end of the year.

These are just some examples of course, and there's a lot of ways which you can go about this based on what your values and priorities may be. If you're really struggling with this and you don't know what your priorities are just yet, don't worry, there is always a solution to work around it. If you need some guidance until you've found your footing and you've got a better idea of what your financial values and priorities are, you could begin your minimalist budget using the 50/20/30 system.

With the 50/20/30 system, you're going to allocate 50% of your income towards meeting your monthly needs. 20% of your income is then going to go towards your savings and paying off your debt, while the remaining 30% of your income is going to be allocated towards your wants. When your "wants" is significantly reduced the deeper you go into minimalism, the percentage allocation of that column can be slowly channeled towards growing that 20% savings to an even bigger number. Minimalism is great because it shows us that the key to happiness is not in satisfying our "wants" at all, and to prioritize your experiences over materialism. That is the foundation upon which minimalism is built. This works out great for your finances since the less you spend the more you get to save.

Learning to eliminate the wants becomes easier when you learn to ask yourself do I value this and does this serve my financial priorities and values? If the answer is no, then you know what to do. Let's say for example you're currently looking at spending about $150 to $200 on your monthly hair treatments at the salon because you want to. Once you've decided to embrace minimalism and your values have shifted, you begin to question whether this expenditure is then serving your purpose. How is spending almost $200 a month serving your financial priorities? More importantly, is this contributing to moving closer to the financial future that you want? The answer is going to depend again, on what your priorities and your values are. Some people may say yes, others may say no. if you find that this expense is not fitting in with your new lifestyle as a minimalist, then it is time to scale back and cut it out from your budget. You are setting your minimalist budget for a reason, and it is important that you stick to this budget no matter what. No matter how tempted you may be, remind yourself why you established this budget in the first place, especially during the first several weeks or months when you're only just beginning to transition into minimalist and adjusting to the new lifestyle.

After you have tackled simplifying your monthly expenses with the help of your values, priorities, and goals, it is now time to work on simplifying your accounts and credit cards. How many credit cards do you currently own? One? Two? Four perhaps? What about a savings account? How many accounts do you own? A simple minimalist budget might look towards having just one savings account and only one checking account, and perhaps one credit card for any possible emergency situations where you might need one. Everything else needs to be removed.

You only need one checking account to handle all your monthly expenses and one saving account where you build your financial nest egg. Having only one of each makes it easier for you to focus on where your money is going and it simplifies your banking process too. Similarly, you should only aim to have just one credit card, perhaps even no credit cards at all if you can manage that. It is going to make it much easier for you to track your spending and stay organized on top of your finances when you don't have so many things to focus on at once. It might come as a surprise to know that the reality is, you only need one of each to survive, but think about it. Is there a genuine need to have several checking or savings accounts? Why separate your savings into several different accounts (vacation, emergency, etc)? Having multiple things to organize can turn out to be a very messy system, and if you're one of those people who is constantly borrowing from one account to help you fund another account, keeping track of your expenses becomes more complicated than it needs to be. A jack of all trades becomes a master of none, and diversifying your savings into several different savings accounts leaves you with barely anything in the multiple accounts you hold.

Consider starting your minimalist budget with just one account each for checking, savings, and retirement. It keeps your finances extremely simple, makes saving money much easier, and makes it easier to organize your budget when your finances aren't spread out all over the place.

Another great approach which minimalists take to simplify their budget and spending is to automate as many of their payments as possible. Anything that can be automated, do it! Automate your savings to be directly deposited into your savings and retirement accounts, automate your debt payments and your bill payments. This is going to make it much easier for you to stay on top of all your payments so you avoid those pesky late payment charges.

Creating a minimalist budget is also going to require that you look back at all your past spending habits and purchases, which will then allow you to question any future purchases you are going to make from this point forward. It is important to do an honest evaluation of just what your spending was so you could determine a pattern or spending habits. Getting to know your spending habits better will lead you to identify when you might be lapsing back into your old ways. It is just as important to question all your future purchases by asking the question you already know is coming - is this necessary for me? It took you a long time to earn the money that you are now thinking about spending, so every purchase you make needs to count and be worth that time and effort spent earning those dollars.

After successfully establishing a budget for yourself, there is one final part of the process that needs to be taken care of, setting up a regular financial meeting with yourself so you can review your progress. Getting organized, simplifying your finances and setting a successful budget is one thing, but maintaining and implementing it effectively over time is another. There will be changes in your life along the way, which means there is never going to be a perfect plan or a budget that you create just once and you're set for life. A constant and regular review of your budget is essential to keeping up with your finances, making sure that this budget still works for you. Regular reviews also give you the opportunity to make any changes or needed tweaks to your budget to make it work better. Start by committing to at least one day out of the week where you revisit your budget and expenses for the week. Observe how well you have managed to stick to what you committed to, and how much progress you've made so far.

CHAPTER 6
Decluttering the Digital

Who would have thought that minimalism would extend to decluttering your computer and other digital aspects of your life too? It is amazing how much of our lives can actually be simplified if we think about it. You may be asking yourself why there is a need for digital decluttering. Why would you need, for example, to declutter your computer when it seems to be working just fine right now? Computers need to be decluttered just as much as the rest of our lives because having too many things stored on it is only going to slow it down gradually. Not to mention how too much clutter is going to leave you with very little space to store your files if you don't clean out your system every now and then.

Having a digital cleanup routine can be just as beneficial as having a physical cleanup routine. Just because the clutter on your digital devices may not be as evident or visible as the ones directly in your environment, that doesn't mean it doesn't exist. The clutter will still be there, building up file after file, document after document, and we don't even realize it until we start to wonder one day why our devices don't seem to be performing as optimally as they should.

Digitally decluttering is not just about saving space and making your devices work faster though, it is also about enhancing your productivity. We give very little thought to the fact that the clutter we see every day on our phones and our computers is actually an invisible killer that squashes your productivity levels. The way your desktop is set up right now has an invisible impact on you mentally. Too much going on causes you to be easily distracted, and instead of jumping onto an urgent task right away as soon as your computer starts up, you idle and linger for several minutes looking at all the other stuff that's going on before getting started on the task you should have begun 10-minutes ago. How often has this happened to you?

Do You Put As Much Effort Into Digital Decluttering?

How much time and effort do you spend digitally decluttering? Once in a while? Frequently? Almost never? If you do conduct the occasional cleanup, do you think you're putting in the same amount of effort on this digital cleanup as you do for the physical decluttering process? Digital clutter may not be as problematic as physical clutter, but it is troublesome nonetheless, and the thing is, you will never be able to eliminate it entirely the way that you can with physical clutter because of how much our lives are now tied to the digital space. Whether we like it or not, technology isn't going anywhere anytime soon, and in fact, we seem to be getting more dependant on it now more than ever. Since it isn't possible to completely eliminate this kind of clutter, the best thing you could do for yourself is to learn how to simplify it so navigation becomes easier.

Digitally Decluttering Leads to Better Productivity

Modern man relies so heavily on their digital devices. From the moment we wake up to the time we lay our heads down on the pillow at night, our lives are intertwined throughout the day with the digital space. Computers, laptops, mobile phones, tablets, even smartwatches are supposedly here to simplify our lives and make things easier so we spend less time on our workload, but it has become quite the opposite. That's because if the lifestyle that we lead is already naturally cluttered, to begin with, this tends to carry over onto our digital lives too. All the extra "hours" you supposedly would have gained from quicker and faster internet processes have now been lost wading through mountains of emails that need to be sorted out, searching for documents online, and of course, countless hours spent aimlessly browsing through social media apps.

Leonardo Da Vinci once said that simplicity is the ultimate sophistication, and he was right. Clutter is nothing but a distraction, not to mention how unappealing it looks visually. Here's what the computer of a minimalist might look like (this is going to be different for everyone based on your needs). Think of a desktop which is clean, clutter-free and perhaps even emptied folders. All you see when you log in is the image that you have chosen as your desktop wallpaper. A simple, minimalist approach which helps them to immediately focus on what needs to get done for the day without the distraction of unnecessary folders vying for their attention. A completely empty desktop with no icons is simplicity at its finest. Every minimalist might have a different approach to it which works for them of course, but this is just an example of-of what their computer might look like.

Minimalists choose to purposely not have a cluttered desktop, despite the fact that it may seem easier to have your most frequently used apps or documents on it so you can quickly access them with a simple double-click. It may be easier, but there's a reason why minimalists choose not to do this. It's because having too much going on and let it be the first thing that you see when you sign onto your computer causes visual distraction and stress. Imagine logging onto your laptop and seeing nothing on the screen but a simple, calming picture that you've chosen as your desktop wallpaper. Now, imagine logging on and seeing about 20 different folders and documents all at once on your screen, just screaming reminders at you about how much work needs to get sorted through. Which is going to be the one that causes you the most stress? A simple tweak, but one that makes a big impact on your mental and emotional state of being.

Minimalists instead choose to organize all the icons on their desktop into a folder. All the documents and folders that currently sit on your desktop right now as the very first step, and you can sort through them later. Once you've cleaned that up, you can begin working on creating separate folders according to your document needs, labeling each folder "Work", "Pictures", "Contracts", and anything else you might need. Every document should have a "home", which is a folder, of its own. Transfer all of these documents onto your computer's hard drive and store them there instead of the desktop.

Once you've done that, it is time to pick your desktop wallpaper. It is important to stick to the theme of minimalism, even when choosing your wallpaper. Keep it simple, clean, serene, calm and peaceful. A quick search on Google will reveal plenty of minimalist wallpaper options to choose from. Plain colors or perhaps a nice, serene nature scene might work. As long as your wallpaper doesn't have too much going on that it becomes distracting.

It is entirely possible to streamline the digital aspects of your life, and you can accomplish this by going through the following steps:

- **Decluttering Your Social Media** - The number one distraction and productivity killer these days are social media. Facebook, Instagram, Twitter, SnapChat, Pinterest and more take up far too much of our time as we spend scrolling and searching without any real purpose or intention. You tell yourself you're only going to check these social media apps for a couple of minutes, but the next thing you know half an hour has gone by and you've fallen behind on a task you should have started. Decluttering begins with your social media apps, and it's time to work through them one by one. You don't need to delete your accounts, but you do need to start thinking about downsizing in terms of your connections and who you follow. Facebook friends that you barely know or haven't had a real conversation with in years don't need to be on your list, delete them. This one action alone makes a tremendous impact on your newsfeed and the less material you have to scroll through, the less time you're going to spend online. Do the same thing across all your other social media platforms. Your social media connections should only be limited to the few important people in your life to keep it meaningful. Remove everyone whom you rarely have a connection with to streamline your experience.
- **Downsizing Email Time** - It was mentioned in Chapter 3 about how you should consider downsizing to only have one email account. Or perhaps two, if you want to keep your office email address and personal email separate. How many email accounts do you currently own besides the one you need to use at the office? You don't need to have Gmail, Yahoo Mail or Hotmail

simultaneously; there is no real need for multiple email accounts. Pick just one email account to work with and eliminate the rest. Once you have done that, it is time to assess your email content and streamline your inbox. Unsubscribe to emails which you no longer have any interest in. Emails which are not relevant, beneficial or impacting your life in any major way does not need to stick around. All those subscription emails reminding you about the latest promotions and sales are unnecessary distractions and they make your inbox look messy. Hit the unsubscribe button. Next, work on your email content and delete anything that is no longer relevant to you. For the emails that you do need to keep, create separate folders to organize these emails according to content. Your main email home page should only contain new emails which come in daily and nothing more. By streamlining and eliminating the unnecessary, you will then be able to work on minimizing the amount of time spent on emails. For personal emails, make it a point to only check it twice a day at most, once in the morning and once at night. Aim to spend no more than an hour responding and catching up on emails. Work emails should be kept during work hours only, and anything else that takes place after hours can be left until tomorrow unless extremely and absolutely of utter importance. We're talking urgency like your career is on the line. If it isn't then emails are not a priority and they can wait.

- **Purging Your Mobile Phone** - If you managed to successfully declutter your computer, tackling your mobile phone next should be a walk in the park. Of course, some might still find this challenging, having to delete the apps on their phone, and it might seem odd at first to have your phone screen looking surprisingly empty and vacant. Once you get used to the simplicity of it all though, you'll wonder why you didn't get on this sooner because of how much easier it has made going through your mobile phone. Begin by going through your current apps and removing anything that you no longer need, want to use. Your home screen should only contain the apps which are of utmost importance to you, and the ones that you frequently use every single day. Would it amaze you to find out that having just one page for all your apps is completely possible? Consider purging your contact list too, deleting any numbers that you no longer have any use for. The most important numbers are going to be those of your family and friends anyway and really, that's all you need when you get right down to it. That, and a couple of important contact numbers and details from work. That is all your contact list should contain. Repeat the same steps for your other digital devices.

You never know just how easy and hassle-free your life can be until you begin to streamline and organize it, and that's why minimalists love this concept so much. Suddenly, they have more free time on their hands to do the things they love and to spend it with the people they love when they're no longer bogged down by all the unnecessary. Reducing your screen time may seem like an impossible thought, but once you make a conscious effort to do so, you're going to see a big difference. Far too many of us are too caught up with technology, allowing it to run our lives and rob us of precious quality time.

Other Strategies to Help You Digitally Declutter

Other helpful strategies and approaches which you could take to digitally declutter include:

- Avoid using your desktop as the default "save" location for all your items. Remember how every item in your home has a "home" of its own? Create "homes" for your important documents by sorting them into folders.
- Set reminders to prompt you when it's time to clean things up.
- Don't download unnecessary apps that you don't need. Remember the minimalist way; everything must have a purpose, an impact, and a benefit. If it doesn't, then you don't need it.
- Streamline your push notifications by turning off the unnecessary ones and only keeping the important notifications turned on. You don't need notifications from your social media apps, they're only distracting you. Notifications should only come from text messages and important reminders.
- Turn off your personal email notifications; you don't need them to be turned on all day. Controlling how many emails you receive in a day will significantly cut down your screen time.
- Track down the documents which are wasting space on all your digital devices right now and consider either getting rid of them or storing them digitally in the cloud instead. These documents could sneakily be taking up space on your computer, and if you haven't used them for so long you even have forgotten that you have them, then it's a safe bet that you could probably remove them for good.
- It is time to unplug and deactivate all those online accounts you no longer use. You've probably signed up for dozens of services and accounts online, some which you have long forgotten about but still keep receiving emails from. If you can't even remember your login details and passwords to those accounts, why still keep them around? Streamline your online life by ridding yourself of anything and everything that is unnecessary.
- Unfollow groups and pages on Facebook that you are no longer interested in, especially if it's not relevant to you anymore. Remember, social media should be kept for only keeping in touch

with people, and perhaps some companies or groups that you genuinely have an interest in or care about.
- If you don't know someone on social media immediately, consider rejecting their friend request. You don't need to have 500 people on your friend's list if those people are not people who matter to you. Quality over quantity is something which can be extended towards your social circle too. Having only 10 quality contacts on your social media is much better than having 100 that are of little significance to you.
- If Facebook is reminding you that it is someone's birthday today but you don't feel any inclination to reach out and send them a quick birthday message, that's a good sign that it could be time to remove them as a friend. If they were someone important, or someone who mattered a great deal to you, you will always want to reach out on special occasions.

Going Paperless

Going paperless is something that is going to be another big adjustment for many. Particularly, if you have been so used to relying on paper documents and hard copies to get you by all this time. But that old fashioned system of having files and drawers crammed full of paper is nothing but clutter. With the busy and hectic lives that most of us live these days, having to sort through all these documents and files is going to be a very time-consuming process, and we simply don't have that kind of time to waste, especially for minimalists. Simplify and declutter your filing process by not filing your documents. That's right, stop the filing process. Everything can be stored online on digital drives these days, and there is really no longer any need for having paper hard copies these days. Even contracts and important documents are now being sent electronically.

G-Drive, DropBox and even iCloud have made it so easy, quick and efficient to drag and drop your files, uploading them to the cloud in a matter of minutes. The best part is how they don't occupy any physical space in your environment at all. Clutter-free! Even better is that you can access these files when they're stored online from anywhere you may be, as long as you have a strong internet connection and a digital device to log into your account. No more having to travel back and forth lugging heavy important documents which you might misplace or lose anyway, which makes the cloud option the safer choice. The files will be there forever, and you don't have to worry about losing them the way that you would with physical copies of these documents.

If you want even more protection and peace of mind (because you happen to be one of those people that constantly worry about losing your files if your digital devices happen to crash), you could always back up your documents on an external hard drive as a safety measure too. Filing all your documents online is the simplest approach that makes the most sense. You can quickly and easily sort and locate any document that you need within a matter of minutes, thanks to the search function that these online storage systems provide. The search feature is even available on your laptop, and this beats spending unnecessary time having to sort through physical copies of documents trying to find what you're looking for any day of the week.

Even your pictures can be stored online quickly and conveniently, eliminating the need for physical photo albums which only take up space in your home. All the pictures that we take are done through our mobile phones these days anyway, so why not take it a step further and store them online too? Save your pictures in the cloud and like the documents, you will be able to quickly and easily access them anytime, anywhere.

We all live in a digital world these days, so really we need to start asking ourselves why is there still a need for so much paperwork in our lives? Especially in our offices, some people may still be reluctant to make the change, simply because they're so accustomed to having physical hard copies that they can hold in their hands. It gives them a sense of security, being able to hold these physical copies for themselves, and the push to go digital is going to take a bit of time for them to get used to the idea. Transferring all your paperwork to the digital space is going to take some time to sort through, but then so was decluttering your home. That probably took you a long time to work through but look at how beneficial it turned out to be now that you did it. Well worth the effort, wouldn't you say? The same thing goes for your digital documents.

Think of how much lighter and freer you would feel in your home office and your work office without all that paper cluttering and taking up space on your desk and shelves. Going paperless is not as challenging as you might initially think, and to begin, you simply need to begin questioning your existing documents. For every note, form, and paper, ask yourself if this document is something that you are going to need long term and if it is, can it be made digital. The answer is going to be yes or no, of course, depending on the type of document you have. A post-it note reminding you about to pick up some bread and milk afterward, for example, does not need to be made digital because you're not going to need it again. An important document like your employment contract, for example, is something that can be made digital (if it isn't already) because this is an important document which you're going to need to hold onto for some time.

Another way of going paperless is to simply stop printing everything out. Read them on your computer, tablet or mobile phone. If you're only going to print them out to read and then toss in the recycling bin when you're done, that's a waste of valuable resources (minimalists care about the environment, remember?). Other ways to cut down on your paper trail include:

- Avoid sending faxes, because they are outdated anyway since everything can easily be emailed or shared across the cloud.
- Avoid sending letters and memos, emails are the more sensible approach, and you don't waste any resources doing it.
- If you rely on the use of forms at work, consider transferring these forms online and getting people to fill them out there instead.
- Send digital invoices instead of paper invoices. There is plenty of software available that allows you to quickly create digital invoices in mere minutes.
- Switch to using contracts online instead of printing out physical copies and manually mailing it to the receiving party. It is easy to sign contracts digitally these days.
- Checks are an outdated system of payment, everything is done online these days anyway.
- Cut back on your paper magazine subscriptions and switch to online subscriptions instead. Almost all newspapers and magazines are available digitally these days.

CHAPTER 7
Living With A Non-Minimalist

Living with people can sometimes be a challenge on its own, but doing it whilst also being a minimalist? That's probably going to be twice or three times the challenge. Your journey towards minimalism is going to come with a series of challenges, one of which is going to be skepticism and doubt you're going to receive from others. They could be your family, your friends, children, roommates, even your colleagues at work who have noticed you furiously cleaning out your cubicle in a decluttering spree and wonder what on earth you were doing. Even harder when the doubt and hesitation usually come from the person who would normally be your biggest supporter, which in this case would be your spouse. The one you're living with.

Suddenly your biggest and most dedicated supporter is going to be the one who becomes the greatest challenge, especially when they find it hard to see why you've chosen to go down this road and completely change everything the two of you have become so comfortable with as you built your life together. It can be hard when the person that you love the most doesn't seem to grasp the benefits and see things from your point of view, and it could take a long time and a lot of convincing before you can successfully get them on their side. You might even have to brace yourself for the fact that they might never fully embrace minimalism because it simply isn't something that they want. That could be a very tough pill for you to swallow if you're so used to doing everything together. To make matters even more difficult, the two of you are living together, sharing one space, and all the stuff that comes with that space.

Whether it is your roommate, friends or your spouse, living with someone is not always going to be smooth sailing all the way. When you decide to make a life change for yourself, you have to brace for the fact that they might not always be on board or supportive of what you're planning to do. You may think that you are making the best decision in the world, while they might see it as you're doing something totally insane trying to give away more than half of your belongings. The transition to minimalism is going to involve a lot of change, and when there are other people in the mix who are not going down the same path that you are, adjustments need to be made.

The Survival Guide to Living With Loved Ones Who Are Not Minimalists

You may not always see eye-to-eye with your family (if you're living with more than just your spouse in your household), but there are several things you could do to help make the transition into minimalism easier not just for them, but for yourself too.

- **Respecting Decisions** - It is important to respect everyone's decision in this scenario, even if their decision may not be something you agree with or what you hoped for. Trying to force everyone to go along with your lifestyle when they are not prepared for it (or want to do it) is going to create a lot of tension and arguments in the relationship. If your spouse, children or roommates are not ready to be on board with your decision to be a minimalist, respect their decision and let them be.
- **Seeing Is Believing** - Sometimes, the most effective approach that you can take would be to let others see for themselves just how beneficial becoming a minimalist can be. Since they are living with you, they are bound to notice the positive changes which are taking place in your life, especially when you're happier than you were before. Not only are they going to see it, but this new, happier, positive energy is going to rub off on them too, and they'll eventually start to see that you might be onto something with this whole minimalist living approach. Who knows, they might even like it enough and want to reap the same benefits they see you experiencing and try it out for themselves too.
- **Avoid Being Defensive** - It can be frustrating when you're trying to convince others to see things from your point of view and they're not being supportive. Sometimes they might even be critical and naturally, you feel like you want to defend your decisions and your choices. You're going to have to make some hard decisions as a minimalist when it comes to your belongings in particular, and your spouse, family or kids might even question you constantly about the choices you're making. Don't let that get you bent out of shape, and instead of being defensive, try to calmly explain your decisions and provide them with as much information as possible. Remember that they don't understand why you're doing this, and their questioning it to find some answers to help them make sense of it all. It is not a direct attack on you in any way.
- **Regular Discussions** - It is important to have regular discussions with your spouse and family about the decision that you make as a minimalist. This helps everyone find common ground and compromise, which is a huge part of ensuring that everyone is happy at the end of the day. It is important to learn how to work together for the long term, because this is going to be a lifelong journey, and you don't want your family to be unhappy along the way.
- **Talking About Your Progress** - As you progress, talk to your family about each step that you take so they know what's happening every step of the way. At each stage of the decluttering process when it comes to common and shared spaces, you may

need to explain why and where you are in the minimalist process. Talk to them about what you intend to do before you clear space, whether their belongings are involved or not, and once they understand and agree, go ahead with your progress.
- **Creating Organized Spaces** - If you happen to live with someone who's a collector, a good compromise would be to help them create an organized space in the home where they can store these items. When you declutter, you're not going to be able to get rid of their collectible items if they're not ready to let these things go. That's just going to cause an argument between the two of you. You're not going to be able to stand the items being strewn about in a disorganized manner either since this is not going to be aligned with your new minimalists' values. Compromise and find common ground to work it by talking things through and helping them create an organized space they would be happy with displaying their items, and you get to be happy not having "clutter" around your home.
- **Avoid Assumptions** - Don't assume that your spouse, family members or roommates are going to automatically know what's going on or what you're up to. You may know what you're doing and what's required as part of your journey towards minimalism, but that doesn't necessarily mean that they understand it. You know why you're decluttering the bookshelf, but that doesn't mean they do. Assumptions may lead to misunderstandings and arguments, and you want to avoid that by reminding yourself that your family may not always understand the decisions behind your actions. Avoid assuming and always seek to clarify instead.
- **Explain the Benefits** - The benefits of minimalism may have got you all excited and eager to begin, but for your family who has no idea what this concept entails, let alone how beneficial it can be, they're not going to understand why you decided to do a complete 180-degree change. To them, there is nothing wrong with the way they're currently living, and they're not going to see a need for anything to change. It is up to you to explain the benefits of this new approach you have decided to go with, and to let them know how you believe it is going to help you. If you believe minimalism is going to make you feel calmer, let them know. If you believe minimalism is going to be beneficial for your finances, let them know. If you believe it is going to help you reconnect with what's important in your life, let them know.
- **See Their Side of Things** - As much as you want them to see things from your perspective and why you believe minimalism is something you should embark on, it is equally important that you see things from their perspective too. It may be hard for you to understand why nobody seems to be seeing the benefits the same

way that you do, but likewise, they will have a hard time understanding why you don't see how upset these changes may cause them to feel. You're about to change everything they have become so accustomed to, and getting rid of a lot of things in the home which they may have formed attachments to. Imagine if someone in your family suddenly decided that they want to get rid of stuff around the home, a lot of which may be your stuff which you like. That's not going to be something you're automatically okay with. Empathize with them and put yourself in their shoes and it will make the process much less stressful on yourself and them.

- **Set an Example** - You can't force someone to go along with what you want, but you can set an example for them to follow. When someone is having a tremendously positive effect on your life, the changes are going to be hard to miss. Your family is bound to notice eventually, and slowly they'll start warming up to the idea, possibly even consider jumping on board the minimalist concept with you. Being a good example is especially important if you have young children in your home. They observe, notice and copy everything that you do, even the things you think they may not be paying attention to. It is through the example that you set where they are going to learn true happiness doesn't come from material possessions. Be the best example that you can be, and they will eventually come around.
- **Don't Force Change On Them** - You can't force someone to change if they're not ready for it. The desire to change needs to come from within, and it is never going to work if they feel like they are being forced into doing something they don't want to. You may think that you're doing them a huge favor by helping them declutter their home, but that is not how they are going to feel. You would feel angry if someone just tossed out your stuff without talking to you about it first, and it is only natural that they would feel the same way. If they're not ready for it, don't force them into it.
- **Don't Let Stuff Come In Between** - At the end of the day, they are just stuff, and the last thing you want is for it to let it come in between your relationship. Don't forget that minimalism is about holding onto and focusing on what matters the most, and the relationships that you have with the people you love will always win over any amount of stuff, any day. If you're frustrated that your spouse or family is getting in the way of your decluttering process because they want to hold onto something that you want to get rid of, allow yourself to feel frustrated, but don't hold it against them. Learn to let go of those feelings quickly by

reminding yourself you can work on finding a compromise later and move on.
- **Start With Your Own Stuff First** - Since minimalism was your idea to begin with, it is only fair that you work on clearing your own stuff first before moving onto theirs. True, the outcome may not be as effective as you would have hoped, seeing as how you might only have been able to clear away a portion of what you would have liked to, but it's better than nothing. You need to start somewhere, so start by working on purging your own stuff first. Perhaps when they see how much better the house looks without as much clutter around, they'll want to get in on the decluttering process too. True, it is easier to notice someone else's mess first before you even notice your own, but that's what you're going to need to do if you want to make this arrangement work.
- **Don't Be Discouraged If They Don't Like It** - Not everyone is always going to like or want to do the same things as you. That can be disappointing, but don't let that discourage you if they don't like minimalism as much as you wanted them to. You chose to be a minimalist because you believed it would benefit you and make you a better person for it, and that's the motivation that you need to remind yourself of whenever you feel yourself losing heart.
- **Ask them to Help** - They may not be on board with becoming 100% minimalist just yet, but you can still ask for their help to keep the home neat and tidy after you have decluttered what you could. Sit them down for a chat and tell them you worked very hard to get the home neat and clean again, and you would appreciate it if they could support you by helping to put things away in their proper place to keep the home clutter-free. Young children might need a little bit more explanation and guidance with this one, but again lead by example and they will eventually copy what you do. Let them know that you have given every item in the home a "home" of its own, and if they could help you out by returning these items to their "homes" whenever they can, that would make you very happy.

It may not always be easy living with someone who isn't a minimalist or on board with what you're doing, but there are certain things that you can do to help make the living arrangements easier. The most important thing to remember is to constantly communicate every step of the way so neither party gets caught off guard by what is happening. If someone is unhappy with something, talk about it and try to find a workable solution you will both be happy with.

Above all else, be patient with them. They are still your family at the end of the day, and nothing is worth compromising on that relationship. One day of decluttering the bookshelf, living room or closet is not going to immediately inspire them to start picking up minimalism right away. Be patient and keep doing what you're doing, they'll eventually come around and be supportive of your efforts when they see how much better and happier you are.

How to Now Deal With Your Other Loved Ones Who Are Not Minimalists Either

Deciding to become a minimalist and live a simpler, happier and more meaningful life can be a very exciting prospect. For the people who decided that this is what they want to do. Everyone else is going to simply look at you with confusion and wonder why on earth you would suddenly decide to give away half your stuff and think that you could be happier without them. You can't blame them for feeling this way, and after all, you might even have felt that way for a long time. This is what most have us have grown up with all our lives, being surrounded by the consumerist lifestyle, and many people don't know any other way of life.

Undergoing this change is very exciting for you because you have now seen the light, but all your other loved ones might have it difficult to understand your decision and how this is going to affect them. You are about to embark on a new life-changing journey that is supposed to strengthen your relationships and bring you closer to the people you love, but when you're going through changes that they don't always understand, it can be hard to feel the close connection with them during the difficult transition. Here's what you can do to make it a little bit easier on yourself.

- **Know That You Might Have to Explain Yourself** - You might not like having to do it, but in this case, you probably have to consider making an exception. Other family members, friends, and even colleagues (since you'll be decluttering your office too) are going to have some comments. Maybe even a lot of comments. Some of these comments and remarks might rub you the wrong way, even if they did not intend for it to be. What you're doing is going to be something that they're not used to, perhaps never even heard of, and they're going to have a lot of questions, comments and perhaps even suggestions about it. Why are you doing this? What are you going to do with all your stuff? Why do you need to give it away? Is this going to change who you are? Some of your loved ones and friends might even have concerns about whether this is going to impact the relationship that they have with you, and the best thing you could do to assuage all those fears is to take the time to explain what you're doing and why. Explain all the ways in which minimalism is going to benefit you. Explain what the process involves. Explain what you're going to do with all your stuff. Explain how this is going to improve your relationship when you're no longer distracted.

- **Thank Those Who Are Being Supportive** - Some family and friends will immediately be supportive and have your back no matter what. These people are the true stars because they never judge the decisions that you make and instead do their best to support you in any way that you might need. They will still be curious about what you're doing, but to those who love and care about you the most, your happiness is all that they need to get them on your side. They serve as reminders of why you're choosing to do this, so you can now turn your focus towards these precious relationships because they bring you more happiness than buying a new jacket or a new pair of shoes ever could. They respect your choices and they don't belittle you for them, even if those choices are not something they would have chosen for themselves. Take a moment to truly thank them for their support and let them know how much it means to you on this journey.
- **Be Honest** - Hiding bits and pieces of information or trying to do things under wraps has never panned out long-term. Besides, you're not going to be happy if you have to hide parts of who you are from your loved ones because you think they might not understand what you're doing. Honesty will always be far and away, the best approach to take, even more so in times like this when you're about to make a big change in your life. Answer any questions that come your way with complete honesty. It is okay if not everyone is going to agree with you.
- **Highlight the Positive Sides** - The biggest question that most people are going to ask is - why you're doing it, and when they do - highlight the positives more than the challenges. It's not about trying to convince them by only talking about the good things, but it's because challenges are not going to last forever, whereas the benefits that you are going to get out of this experience will last you a lifetime. So why dwell on something that is only a small bump in the road in the grand scheme of things? Talk about the positives to help others see where you're coming from, like how minimalism has made you happier because you now have more time to spend with the people you love and pursue the things that you love.
- **Avoid Sounding Preachy** - Phrases like "you should" or "you must" are going to make you sound preachy, and make it seem as though you're trying to push your new lifestyle onto the rest of your family. Rubbing your loved ones the wrong way by trying to be too pushy is only going to turn them off to the idea of minimalism instead of helping them to understand and embrace the choice that you have made.
- **Learn to Adopt a Sense of Humor** - You might get a few jokes thrown your way, and some of your friends might resort to teasing

you about what you're doing. Adopting a sense of humor approach is going to help you learn to take it in stride instead of taking it personally. They usually don't mean any harm by it, and family and friends always tease each other at a comfortable level anyway. If you're feeling sensitive about the comments because you're still working through these changes yourself, learn to see the funny side of things and smile or laugh along with them.

- **Avoid Taking Things Negatively** - Not every comment that is being said is done out of spite or with a negative intention behind it. True, your loved ones and friends may not be on the same wavelength as you about this subject right now, but avoid assuming that everything they are saying or doing is associated with negativity. They could just be making a general comment or observation with no malicious intent behind it. If you're not sure, it doesn't hurt to clarify things with them instead of jumping to your own conclusions and getting mad at them.

Change is always going to be difficult, even if it is for the best. Explaining the change is possibly even harder when you're trying to convince someone else to see where you're coming from. The best thing you could do for yourself is to give them some time to adjust, they'll get used to it eventually, just like how you need some time to get used to your new life too.

CHAPTER 8
Traveling Light

You got your suitcase ready for your vacation and you're ready to start packing. As your suitcase starts filling up, you begin to wonder if it's going to be enough. Perhaps you need another for all the stuff you can't quite fit into this one? But then is one more going to be enough? Maybe you should pack a dressier piece of clothing in case you might need it. Or maybe a couple more pairs of shoes so you've got some options to work with. Do you need a raincoat or a lightweight jacket? Maybe both? Suddenly one suitcase becomes two or three pieces of luggage that you're carting around with you and to the airport. Does this sound just a little too familiar?

Packing light seems to be a struggle for many. How do those backpackers and travelers on YouTube seem to fit everything that they need for three weeks or more into just a backpack? That almost seems like magic when you're struggling to fit even one week's vacation worth of items into a medium-sized suitcase. You end up with all sorts of items you never initially planned on bringing with you but decided to at the "last minute" just in case you might need them. The "just in case" scenario often never happens, and you're carrying a heavier load than you should for nothing. Minimalism isn't just sweeping into people's homes and their lives anymore, it is taking the travel world by storm too, as more travelers find even more ways to whittle down the items that they carry to the bare minimum that is needed for them to survive comfortably on their trip. Most backpackers and travel bloggers especially have become experts at carrying just one piece of luggage with them, a miraculous feat which leaves the rest of us speechless and wondering is that all they packed?

A quick search online will lead you to several videos and posts where minimalist travelers talk about how liberating it is to be able to travel quickly and efficiently without anything weighing or slowing them down. With everything that they need all in just one backpack or suitcase, moving around at the airport and in between cities has never been easier. Nothing feels unnecessary or superfluous, and they feel much happier traveling because none of the stress which is associated with over packing or lugging around heavy baggage is a problem they have to deal with.

Minimalist Travel Explained

By now, you would already be familiar with the resonating theme in minimalism, which is to only have what you need and nothing more. This concept is now going to carry over towards your travel habits, whereas a minimalist traveler, you're going to pack only the absolute necessities, and not a scrap of clothing or item more. When you can fit your entire life into a mere backpack or suitcase, then you know you're doing something right.

By right, traveling as a minimalist should enable you to travel the world for a year and still be able to survive with just one bag alone. By limiting yourself to just one piece of luggage, it is going to discourage you from the urge to buy souvenirs and knick-knacks that you're never going to use for long, just for the sake of being able to tell people where you got them. When someone gives you a souvenir, do you really put it to good use? They're probably doing the same thing to the souvenirs that you bring them too. There's really not much you can do with a decorative piece of item with just the name of the destination printed on it.

Minimalist travel encourages you to seek out simplicity over the need for luxury, to put more emphasis on the experiences that you gain rather than the hotel you're staying in or how much you could buy and bring home with you. Minimalism is encouraging you to be efficient in every aspect of your life, even travel.

The society that we live in today places far too much emphasis on material possessions. The homes that we live in are a reflection of us, and many people dream of owning a big, luxurious home because they believe it is a reflection upon the success they have achieved. We buy expensive cars we can't afford because we want to show the rest of the world that we can have them. We seem to desire things rather than personal needs, focusing on what we can buy next instead of focusing on our health, relationships or passion. To put it plainly, the things that we own matter more to us than they really should. Our homes may be filled, but our hearts continue to remain empty - the only thing that can fix that emptiness, is minimalism.

Once you start adopting minimalism in your home, it won't be long before it spills over into the rest of your life. You start actively seeking out other areas of your life where you can rid yourself of excess "baggage", quite literally when it comes to travel.

To become a minimalist traveler, you're going to have to learn how to differentiate between what you want and what you need. For example, you may want to pack your hair straightener and bring it with you on your holiday, but it may not be something that you need if you can survive a week without having to straighten your hair. You may want to pack a pair of heels because you're so used to wearing them in your daily life, but you don't need to pack them because there is rarely going to be an occasion during your travels where you're going to need your heels. Leaving how to separate the "need" from "want" is going to cut down a lot of your travel items just by switching your mindset alone.

Your Guide to Travelling Like a Minimalist

Here's how you get started learning to travel like a minimalist:

Where to Begin

- **Downsizing Your Bag -** In keeping with the spirit of simplicity and downsizing, the first place to start would be to downsize the size of your bag. Instead of a medium or large suitcase, you're now going to get into the habit of only packing a cabin sized bag or even a backpack. You're going to fit one or two weeks worth of items into just a backpack or a cabin sized bag because you decided to do it. How many times have you fallen victim to the "oh I still have space in my bag, I guess I can fit in a couple more items". Not anymore. Becoming a minimalist traveler begins with the intentional choice to choose a smaller bag for your travels and nothing more.

Bonus tip: Consider investing in a lightweight backpack to save your weight limit at the airport.

What's Next?

- **Analyzing Your List** - It's time to downsize your list, and you're going to now analyze every item on your list and ask yourself do you really need this? Which items from your last trip did you bring but ended up not using at all? What non-essential daily habits do you think you could cut from your routine for the next week or two while you're on vacation? Are there smaller or more versatile versions of these items that you plan to bring? Did travel size toiletries for example? Packing is a personal thing, and downsizing your list is going to depend on what you absolutely need to bring with you on this trip and what you can temporarily do without.

- **Your Clothing Color Palette** - With only a few clothing options to your name now that you're a minimalist, getting into the habit of buying items of clothing with a color palette that allows you to easily mix and match your items is going to transform your packing habits like never before. Instead of needing 10 items of clothing to create a week's worth of outfits, you can shave it down to 5 items of clothing and still get a weeks' worth of outfits by mixing and matching your items.

- **Packing Cubes Are Your Friend** - Minimalists are all about keeping things neat, tidy and organized. Not just in their homes, but in their suitcase too. Packing cubes are going to keep your items neatly stored away and easy to find, which makes living out of a suitcase that much easier. Don't you just love the simplicity of minimalism?

Make your life easier by packing clothes which are not only comfortable but don't wrinkle as easily. You might like the idea of creating what's known as a capsule wardrobe, which is where you only choose a few, selected pieces of clothing which you can wear for any occasion and it matches everything that you own. You are always going to have access to shopping places no matter where you go, so if an emergency pops up (which is very rare), you could always quickly run out and get what you need.

Packing and Knowing Your Essentials

You're only going to bring with you what is absolutely needed and necessary while you're on the road. Among the essentials that you absolutely cannot leave home without, for example, include:
- Your passport and travel documents
- Your cash
- Emergency credit card
- Mobile phone and phone charger

These items are at the top of your priority list because you should never leave for a holiday without them.

The second tier of priority items would include the following:
- A lightweight sweater or a jacket
- Toothbrush
- Comfortable shoes
- Only one spare outfit for emergencies
- A water bottle

As long as you've always packed these essentials with you, you could go anywhere and still be okay. Everything else that you need can easily be purchased at your destination.

Minimizing Your Toiletries and Makeup

We've become so accustomed to packing our toiletries for the trips that we take and we have come to think of them as essential items. However, you're not going to need all the toiletries that you think you do. A minimalist would be able to survive with just the following items:
- Soap
- Toothbrush
- Toothpaste
- Deodorant

Lotions, shampoos, and conditioners are optional items because they can easily be picked up at your destination. If you only have a specific preference of shampoo and conditioner and you're not comfortable relying on unknown shampoo brands which might be available where you go, pack travel sized bottles of both to bring with you. Seek all-in-one or multi-purpose items to make traveling even easier if you can just bring one item but use it for several different functions.

Minimizing Your Clothing

Whether you're traveling to a destination with a warmer or colder climate, a minimalist packer can get by with these few staple pieces of clothing:
- One pair of pants (black so it can match all your items of clothing).
- Either one skirt or one pair of yoga pants, depending on your preference for comfort (NOT both).
- 4-5 T-shirts (depending on the length of your travel)
- A lightweight sweater or a jacket (pack both of you're going somewhere where the temperatures can get very chilly)
- 2-4 pairs of underwear (you can wash and wear)

- One sports bra as an additional versatile item
- 1-2 pairs of socks
- An extra pair of shoes
- Bathing suit (depending on your destination)

That's what a basic list of a minimalist traveler might look like. It is going to vary, of course, depending on where you're going, and to help you get the most out of your clothing items, here's what you should keep in mind:
- Always make comfort a priority and pack the most comfortable clothes you have.
- Get used to washing your clothes on your travels, because this is going to remove a lot of clothing items off your list.
- Go with a consistent color palette to easily mix and match your items.
- Only pack shoes you can walk in for hours without breaking a sweat because they'll be your most comfortable pair.

A great tip to remember when it comes to curbing your urge to pack more clothes than you should is to remind yourself of the fact that you're going there for a holiday, not a fashion show. No one is going to be paying attention to the fancy clothes that you wear, and no one is going to notice that you repeat your outfits because guess what? You're not going to be seeing the same people every day. Be as fashionable as you want at home, but keep your holidays simple, free and easy.

Minimizing Your Travel Gadgets

We can't leave home without our tech, but besides your mobile phone and charger (which are technically the only essentials) what else could you shave off your travel list when it comes to electronics? The minimalist traveler can usually only be seen traveling with their:
- Mobile phones
- Phone chargers
- Headphones

And that's it! Since our phones are able to do almost anything our tablets and computers can do these days, there's no need for anything else other than your phone. Some minimalists will choose to bring an extra DSLR camera with them if they're avid photographers who love capturing moments during their travels.

Life Is More Meaningful Beyond the Bag

A minimalist traveler is perfectly happy with a simple backpack and a few pieces of items because they know that it is the experiences they are going to get at their destination which is what really matters. Being a minimalist traveler is going to keep your spending modest too because buying souvenirs and knick-knacks are no longer going to become your priority.

All a minimalist needs to be happy is one piece of light luggage, their plane ticket and travel itinerary, and the excitement of exploring a new destination.

Here are some other great tips to keep in mind that make minimalist travel an even more enjoyable experience:
- If you do happen to make several purchases during your travels (assuming they are absolutely necessary), consider mailing them home if you're still going to be on the road for some time.
- Nothing should be in your pockets except your wallet and your passport. This makes moving through airport security a much quicker process.
- Instead of bringing the entire guide book with you, consider photocopying only the sections that you need to lighten your load. Alternatively, you could just look up the information on your phone.
- Make copies of your important documents, which would be your passport, ID and credit cards or any other valuable documents you may have with you (if you're traveling for business perhaps). Alternatively, you could consider scanning and emailing these documents to yourself so you always have a copy which is easily accessible on your phone.
- It is a good idea to save some emergency contact numbers on your phone and your itinerary where you can easily access it quickly if needed.
- High-tech, quick-drying fabrics are going to be your best friend if you're doing a lot of wash and wear on your journey.
- Avoid over planning your trip, your itinerary should be kept simplified too. Rushing about too much from one place to the next will keep you from enjoying the experience the way that you should.
- Focus on a few meaningful experiences instead of trying to see everything on your trip, which may not always be possible. Quality over quantity at the end of the day, right?
- When traveling to the airport, arriving earlier than you think is necessary will keep you from feeling stressed rushing around hoping that you don't miss your flight.

The Benefits of Travelling Like a Minimalist

Many people would think of minimalist travel as a compromise, when in fact nothing could be further from the truth. When it comes right down to it, it's not about compromise, but efficiency. Plus, aside from having light luggage and only one bag to worry about on your travels, there are several other benefits which come from traveling like a minimalist that will make you wonder why you waited so long to get started:
- **Everything Become Faster** - Going through airport checks and security becomes faster. If you don't have to check in your luggage, the process becomes even faster when you're not wasting time standing in the queues and you can rely on those automated check-in machines and save yourself a lot of time in the process.

- **No More Baggage Claim** - Sail in and out of airports with ease when you no longer have to waste precious minutes waiting at the baggage claim area like everyone else. While all the other travelers are waiting for their bags to emerge, you're already at the airport exit hailing your cab to your hotel. Plus, you avoid dealing with the stress of having your luggage being misplaced or lost in transit.
- **No Worries About Losing Your Bag** - Losing your bag at the airport can be an absolute nightmare. You've arrived at your destination but your bag has not, and there's no telling how soon airport personnel is going to be able to help you sort that out. There's nothing worse than arriving and having to spend extra money and time shopping for all your essentials again. This never has to be an issue again when you learn to travel with just a cabin sized bag or backpack.
- **You're Always First in Line** - Or among the first few people in line at customs and immigration anyway. This is usually where a lot of people get trapped in the bottleneck queues waiting for their turn. By skipping the baggage claim routine, you can ensure that you beat everyone else to the punch, making your airport transitions smooth and as hassle-free as possible.
- **Saving Money on Baggage Fees** - With no checked baggage, you'll save yourself some extra cash, along with the hassle of having to check your bag at the airport. Minimizing your travel gear significantly cuts the expense that comes with overweight baggage. Every airport would have its own requirements and restrictions, and baggage fees are just another added expense which is unnecessary and can easily be removed.
- **Saving Money on Storage** - Let's say you arrive at your destination in the wee hours of the morning and you can't check in just yet because the hotels only have a certain check-in time. With just one bag to contend with, you save yourself some cash not having to pay for bag storage somewhere while you explore the city waiting for your check-in time.
- **Finding Things Is Significantly Easier** - When you've only got the bare minimum with you, you're always able to find exactly what you're looking for within a matter of seconds. Open up your bag and everything you need is right there when you travel like a minimalist. No more wasting time digging around, having to pull out several items to and make a mess rummaging around trying to find what you're looking for.
- **Less Ironing to Contend With** - Especially if you make it a point to pack clothing items which don't wrinkle as easily. Simply wear, wash, dry and wear again. A simple change in your routine which can relieve you of a lot of the travel stress.

- **Your Items Always Match** - You can't go wrong when you've only packed a specific color palette that goes with almost everything and can easily be mixed and matched. No more being caught off guard and suddenly finding yourself with nothing to wear because the items that you have don't go well together and the rest of your clothes are still drying from the wash.
- **You're Always Comfortable** - How could you not be, when you've made it a point to specifically only pack comfortable clothing items? There's nothing that kills a holiday faster than feeling uncomfortable in your clothing, it distracts from the experience when all you want to do is get back to your hotel room and out of your clothes.
- **You're Less Annoyed Overall** - A lot of people tend to underestimate what a stressful experience traveling can be. The long queues, the endless waiting in lines, rushing about from one place to the next, moving through hoards of people trying to get from point A to point B as quickly as possible is not always an easy thing to deal with. By minimizing the complications that you face during your travels, you eliminate a lot of the stress that goes with it too.
- **Packing and Unpacking Can Be Done in Mere Minutes** - The less you pack, the faster you unpack (and pack again when it's time to leave). Some minimalists who have been doing this for a long time can easily be packed and ready to go in 10 to 15 minutes because they have so few items to deal with. Not only does this save a lot of time, but it also gives you peace of mind when you know exactly what items you came with and what you should be left with. When you're not rushing about, you're less likely to leave your stuff behind.
- **Run When You Need To** - Sometimes, no matter how much you plan and prepare, there may be an occasional moment where you might have to sprint through the airport to make it on time. With no wheelie bags or heavy suitcases to contend with, when you need to run, you'll be able to run as you mean it. The lighter your luggage, the faster you move.
- **No Matter Where You Are, You're Set** - Having all the essentials that you need to survive comfortably means that no matter where in the world you go, you're always able to get by because you have all that you need.

CONCLUSION

Thank for making it through to the end of this book, let's hope it was informative and able to provide you with all of the tools you need to achieve your goals whatever they may be.

Minimalism is a simple concept, yet one that can invoke profound change in the lives of those who choose to adopt this approach to living. Less stress, more balance in our lives, a healthier and happier mind, body and soul, all the things that we have struggled to hold onto have been right in front of us all along. We've just been far too distracted by the clutter in our lives to truly appreciate it. Buying new things may make you happy when you do, but that happiness will always be short-lived, and none of it can even come close to the kind of long-lasting happiness that minimalism can bring.

The world we live in may be moving at a rapid pace, but minimalism shows us that we can intentionally slow things down for ourselves by choosing simplicity over clutter in every facet of our lives. Our homes, jobs, relationships, travel, even our devices can be simplified if we wanted. We may not have intentionally chosen the consumerist life we lived before, but we now have a choice to choose something better for ourselves. Because a better life, a simpler, happier life rooted in all the things we value the most is a life worth decluttering for.

Finally, if you found this book useful in any way, a review on Amazon is always appreciated!

DESCRIPTION

Here's to new beginnings.....
A fresh start. A brand new beginning. A change for the better.
Those are all the things so many of us yearn for, but very few fail to accomplish. Why? Because we simply don't know how to go about it in the right way. We have spent most of our lives up to this point believing that our happiness lies in how much we earn, what we own and the things we can buy. We believed that the more we bought, the happier we will be. Yet, how many times have you found yourself returning to those feelings of dissatisfaction, unhappiness, and discontent even after you've bought something you were so sure would make you happy?
On average, almost all of us own more things that we really need to survive. Do you really need to own more than one car if you live somewhere public transport is easily available? Do you really need to own 10 jackets when they all serve the same purpose? Multiple pairs of shoes, some of which you haven't worn in months or even forgotten about? Why do we need to own multiples of the same item when they all serve the same purpose?
Not only is this clutter taking up space in your home, but it is also adding to your stress and you don't even realize it until you wake up to the fact that you could be drowning in your own clutter. It's the time that things started to change for the better, and that change begins with minimalism. Minimalist Mindset is going to walk you through:
- What minimalism is and why you should do it
- How drowning in too much clutter could be holding you back
- The principles that minimalists live by
- Managing your expectations
- Debunking the myths and misconceptions about minimalism
- Getting started on the decluttering process
- How to achieve financial freedom through minimalism
- What it's like to live with a non-minimalist
- How to travel light and travel free

This is the answer to a better way of living you have been searching for all along. This is the key to holding onto that long-lasting happiness which has eluded you for so long. This is your new beginning.

www.ingramcontent.com/pod-product-compliance
Lightning Source LLC
Chambersburg PA
CBHW071407070526
44578CB00002B/512